Advance Praise for *How to Work wit...*

"The methods in this book are unique. It is not a book about how to improve your-self or get along better with others. It is about how to get all those difficult people in your life to be more cooperative. I have used Lucy Gill's model with my clients and it works."

—Robert M. Bramson, Ph.D., author of the bestselling
Coping with Difficult People

"This book is a barnburner: with concise, clear examples, simple steps, and no clutter or jargon. Don't let this book get buried on your 'self-help' shelf."

—Keith Irwin, managing partner,
Tanner-Irwin Management Consultants

"This book is a little gem. It's deceptive in its simplicity. Lucy Gill has managed to translate very new thinking about complicated problems into language that allows the reader to apply the concepts practically in the business world, and be light-years ahead."

—Dr. Richard Fisch, director and principal investigator
of the Brief Therapy Center at MRI, in Palo Alto, CA

"Lucy Gill worked as a consultant in my company and produced great results. She used her methods very productively for us, and I am glad she has written *How to Work with Just About Anyone.* Her humorous and conversational style is like hav-ing her in my office again, kicking ideas around. This is a great book."

—Steven Brown, former president of 800-Software

"Anyone who's ever worked with a frustrating person should read this book. Step by step, Lucy Gill shows how to get even 'impossible' people to change."

—Paul Watzlawick, emeritus clinical professor, Stanford University;
member of the Mental Research Institute, Palo Alto, CA

"With humor and subtlety, Lucy Gill offers a practical method for addressing diffi-cult problems and for successfully getting people to change, and gives you the tools and the confidence to find solutions. Using her methods, we effectively and efficiently resolved very tough conflicts in our company."

—Roland Chazal, industrial vice-president, Perrier Vittel, France

How to Work with Just About Anyone

A THREE-STEP SOLUTION FOR GETTING
DIFFICULT PEOPLE TO CHANGE

Lucy Gill

A Fireside Book /SIMON AND SCHUSTER

FIRESIDE
Rockefeller Center
1230 Avenue of the Americas
New York, NY 10020

Copyright © 1999 by Lucy Gill
All rights reserved,
including the right of reproduction
in whole or in part in any form.

FIRESIDE and colophon are registered trademarks
of Simon & Schuster, Inc.

Manufactured in the United States of America

1   3   5   7   9   10   8   6   4   2

Library of Congress Cataloging-in-Publication Data

Gill, Lucy.
How to work with just about anyone : a three-step solution
for getting difficult people to change / Lucy Gill.
p.   cm.
"A Fireside book."
1. Psychology, Industrial.   2. Interpersonal relations.
I. Title.
HF5548.8.G5327   1999
158.7—dc21   99-27261
CIP

ISBN 0-684-85527-5

BOOK DESIGN BY JENNIFER ANN DADDIO

To my husband, Rich Terrell,
who brings laughter to every day

Acknowledgments

Without Dr. Richard Fisch, director of the Brief Therapy Center at the Mental Research Institute (MRI) in Palo Alto, California, this book would not exist. He invited me to join the center's research team because he was curious about how well their problem-solving model would work in the corporation. Dick, who is a master at simplifying complex problems, patiently taught me their system and worked with me to adapt it to the business world. He read and reread every chapter of this book and offered invaluable advice and encouragement. I can never thank him enough.

I am forever grateful to my sister, Nita Gill, who edited draft after draft with unsisterly patience and whose cheerleading kept me going. Thanks for the priceless writing lessons.

My thanks to Robert and Susan Bramson for their belief in me and in this book, and for their willingness to kick ideas around whenever I got stuck. Bob, my close friend and business partner, was a relentless supporter of this book. His untimely death has cheated the world of a great mind and a gentle man.

My deep appreciation to Felicia Eth, my agent, for taking on this project and for her guidance and support throughout the publishing process.

Thank you to Manuel Diaz, Steve Brown, Brian Gill, Keith Irwin, and Phil Gill who found time in their busy lives to review my manuscript.

Many thanks to Becky Cabaza of Simon & Schuster for her editing expertise, her willingness to listen, and for marshaling the manuscript through the final stages. My thanks to Cherise Grant for her useful comments in the early stages of this book.

I am grateful to Jill Nash, who generously offered her services as a media coach.

Dorothy Jongeward, co-author of *Born to Win*, among other books, invited me into the world of consulting in 1971. I am grateful to her for opening the door to such an intriguing career and for her friendship over the years.

John Weakland, who died in 1995, was an extraordinary listener and an insightful teacher. He gave me the courage to start writing.

My special thanks to my husband, Rich Terrell, who understands the writer's thousand-yard stare and who's always willing to join in the quest for the perfect phrase.

Contents

Foreword

In the competitive business world, problems abound. Lucy Gill addresses those problems encountered in the workplace by people, primarily by those in conflict with one another. This book is about how people frustrate one another in ways that often interfere seriously with the operations of their department, division, or firm. Put simply, it's about how people convert common, resolvable difficulties into full-blown, stalemated problems, and how to resolve those problems. There is a myriad of books addressing these types of problems, but what is different about Lucy's book is that she offers ways to resolve them with *an economy of effort and time.*

She has done a masterful job of laying out the approach clearly, first by giving the reader a full and understandable description of the rationale underlying the subsequent steps: assessing the problem; the strategic "players" in the problem; those factors that maintain and escalate the problem. Then she describes those common notions people hang on to that unwittingly interfere with recognizing alternative and effective solutions; she goes on to show the reader how to overcome those self-imposed roadblocks.

This book is not for the reader looking for inspirational methods or for charming mystifications. Instead, Lucy has painstakingly adhered to down-to-earth descriptions and guidelines that make it easier for the reader to utilize this book easily. It is so forthrightly organized that it barely hints at the sophisticated tools and concepts Lucy has woven into her approach for dealing, efficiently and effectively, with "sticky" problems: recent developments in human communication; advances in rapid problem-solving; and the appreciation of linguistics in the formation of interpersonal conflicts as well as in their resolution.

She is very familiar with the world she is addressing, having been in the "trenches" as a manager and having consulted with organizations for many years. She has embodied that experience in the examples she gives throughout the book, and in the language she uses. This gives the work a "realness" that makes it all the more usable to readers who have an open mind to newer and unique approaches to human problems and who are looking to make changes rapidly.

Richard Fisch, M.D.
January 1999

The Problems That Won't Go Away

If you've ever dreamed—in a weak moment—of herding the exasperating people in your life onto an ice floe and pushing it into a warm sea, this book is for you. I'll show you a simple three-step solution for changing anyone's irritating, offensive, obstructive, lazy, nonproductive, combative, self-serving, infuriating, and otherwise troublesome behavior.

In Section I, you'll see annoying behavior from a new perspective and discover what needlessly prolongs your struggle to change it. You'll learn how to reclaim your appreciable influence over the annoying people in your life, even over a belligerent manager. Then you'll take the first step toward getting your difficult person to change—identify and target the specific trait or habit you want changed.

ONE

The Care and Feeding of Problems: How Difficult Behavior Gets Reinforced

What do you do about impossible people? You know the kind:

- The manager who hands you a rush project and insists that you drop everything to get it done. Then the completed report sits on her desk for a month—just the way it did the last time.
- The ambitious colleague who frequently criticizes your work in front of the boss.
- The otherwise good assistant who is chronically late. She always apologizes, but the excuses are as annoying as her tardiness.

It's the chronic offenders like these who drive you crazy, not the people who occasionally irritate. You can cope with your manager's bad day from time to time. It's when she's having a bad life and taking it out on you that the frustration sets in. When people continue to annoy you no matter what you say or do, that's when you begin to believe that they will never change or that you will never cope—that the troubled relationship (or your job) is doomed.

Not only can you get these people to change their habits, but you can do it with surprisingly little effort *and* without confrontation. Sound impossible? It's not—once you know the right approach. You're about to learn the method that will take the trial and error out of changing anyone's troublesome behavior.

The (Not) Impossible Dream

This method is a result of four decades of research at the Mental Research Institute (MRI) in Palo Alto, primarily the work of the Brief Therapy Center project. In the beginning the founders of MRI studied all types of communication. Then, while analyzing how people handle problems, they discovered that people often get stuck in problems because they pick—and then inadvertently repeat—a solution that doesn't work. Their solution was, in fact, *prolonging* the problem. The researchers figured that the problem would disappear if they: 1) focused on these ineffective solutions rather than on the original problem; and 2) convinced their clients to try something significantly different. So they put aside the traditional diagnostic labels and techniques of psychotherapy and set out to test this hypothesis. Calling their work "brief therapy," the researchers challenged themselves to resolve clients' problems in a maximum of ten one-hour sessions. Over the years they developed and fine-tuned a unique formula that is extraordinarily successful in resolving impossible problems quickly.

Dr. Richard Fisch, John Weakland, and Paul Watzlawick, the senior team members, were curious to see whether their method would be as effective with business problems as it was with the problems of families and individuals. In 1984 I was invited to join the Brief Therapy Center's research team. At that time I had worked for twelve years as a management consultant in a variety of organizations, primarily helping teams function effectively and coaching managers on how to handle difficult and nonproductive behavior. We began to collaborate on business problems, blending the center's techniques with my consulting tools. For instance, if a protracted conflict in an organization was the result of a "systems" problem—like inadequate definitions of people's goals or roles, ineffective communications channels, inappropriate decision styles, or work-flow bottlenecks—then traditional consulting practices sufficed. Remove the cause of friction and the friction ceases. At other times, good management practices were already in place but the conflict persisted, perhaps due to individuals finding each other's habits intolerable. Then the center's three-step model was the better tool. When the cause of the trouble was a combination of these forces, then we used a blend of the methods. In the course of working on a number of problem situations, we discovered that the center's method worked as well with business problems as it had with individual and family difficulties. In fact, the process saved my clients a great deal of time, trouble, and expense.

This book will show you how to use adeptly the three-step process that resolves repetitive problems. You will learn how to:

1. • cut your problem down to size (you'll find that you have less work to do than you thought);
2. • figure out what inadvertently perpetuates your problem (you'll discover how much control you already have); and, based on that,

③ • select a new approach that will get you the change you
want.

These three steps may appear simple, and they are—as simple
as programming your VCR. It's simple, that is, when you've
read the directions. And when you've mastered these three
steps, you'll know how to quickly get people to stop driving you
crazy.

You'll learn some straightforward ways to get people to quit
their annoying habits. You'll also learn some unusual solutions
because, with repeat offenders, common-sense methods often
don't work. For example, it may make good sense to simply ask
your abrasive colleague to stop criticizing you in front of your
boss. It is a logical approach and worth a try. But if it doesn't
work, there is no point in trying it over and over. As you will
learn, a significantly different approach will now be needed if
you want your peer to change. Imagine telling him that you find
his criticism useful and would like him to do it even more, especially in front of your boss. Sounds crazy, but a client of mine
did exactly that and quickly got her peer to back off. You'll
learn how to use such unusual but effective solutions, and many
simpler ones as well.

If you've tried unsuccessfully to change someone's behavior,
you already know what doesn't work. You're about to learn what
does. Here's a preview of the first step in the process: identifying
specifically what behavior needs to change.

Yes, Virginia, People Really Do Change

When repeatedly faced with a manager's or a spouse's irritating
behavior, I have often heard people give up, saying, "What's the

use? People can't change." It's how we console ourselves when we can't get someone to change. In effect, we're saying that our efforts didn't fail, but rather that the irritating person is like the tiger that can't change its stripes. While comforting, it doesn't do much to change those aggravating spouses and thoughtless co-workers.

The fact is, people change all the time. For instance, many of us change our behavior quickly when the CEO walks into the room. We probably behave differently with our colleagues than with our spouses. And it's not likely that we treat each of our children exactly the same (just ask them). We change our behavior all day long. But, you protest, that's not the same as the tiger changing its stripes; however, as you'll see, it's not usually the stripes that need changing.

The problem with saying "people can't change" is that the statement isn't specific. People can't change what, precisely? Let's say that you're frustrated with your hyperactive assistant who is still bouncing off the walls despite your efforts to change him. Before you declare that he can't change, you need to ask yourself: What specifically did you try to change about him? What problem does his hyperactivity create? To succeed at changing him, you have to work on the problem his troublesome behavior creates, not vaguely try to transform his personality. You probably don't really care that he has so much energy; you just wish he'd stop cracking his knuckles, drumming the table, and popping up and down in meetings. In other words, while you can't expect him to become Mr. Mellow, you can get him to stop his constant interruptions in staff meetings. Once you've attacked and fixed the specific problem his hyperactivity creates, you might find the rest of his high energy tolerable. You could even enjoy having him around.

Changing the Changeable

① Clarifying the *specific* problem focuses you on changing the changeable. For example, a friend of mine is a nonstop talker. She can literally go on for hours relating story after escapade after travelogue. She's intelligent and creative and a great story-teller, but I get worn out after hours of listening. I want conversation, not just monologue. One day, after about forty minutes, I interrupted her with a time-out signal and said: "While these stories are entertaining, I really look forward to our conversations—when we kick ideas and theories back and forth. When do we get to do that?" Her response flabbergasted me. "That's what I've been waiting for," she said. I guess while she waited, she was just filling in the empty space with stories.

Obviously my usual method of dealing with her—politely not interrupting, waiting for her to run down—hadn't worked. I have since learned to interrupt and say, "OK. I need conversation now," or in a twist on the old phrase, "Enough about you. Let's talk about me." She then finishes her story and we spend the rest of our visit in satisfying conversation. I've noticed that she has begun to ask me about myself at the start of our time to-gether, making sure I get my turn first, so to speak. I now look forward to seeing her.

Did she change? You bet. She can and does still talk non-stop, but the problem I had with that is resolved. I get to be heard too, we spend a good deal of time in first-rate conversation, and I've learned how to get her to stop when I've had my fill of monologue. Has she altered her style for others? Only for those who have changed their way of dealing with her. For everyone else, I recommend earplugs.

So it's not whether people can change, but whether we can

get people to change what we want them to. After all, even an insufferable boss is nice to someone. The question is not whether that person can change; the question is: How can we make sure *we* are the ones that boss is nice to?

To succeed in getting people to change their irritating behavior, it's useful to recognize what drives people to behave as they do. Once you see behavior from this new perspective, a world of options opens up.

The Predictable Element in "Unchangeable" Situations

When you're struggling to get your manager or co-worker or daughter to change, you probably see your own frustration clearly. But what you might not see clearly is what actually is going on between the two of you—what keeps you from succeeding. It's not easy to step back and observe the show when you're one of the actors. But if you're having trouble getting your manager to change, you can count on two things: 1) your perception of the situation will be quite different from your manager's, and 2) these differing perceptions will complement each other. For instance:

> TOM: "My manager, Murray, micromanages everything. He'll rewrite even the most trivial memo. It's so frustrating. He's got to have the wording his way. So why bother to put in any effort? Now I just send him my first draft and let him have at it!"
>
> MURRAY: "Tom just doesn't care. He would mail out trash if I let him. I've got to check everything, even trivial memos. He has no quality standards. And the more I correct him, the worse he gets."

How frustrating for Murray. The more he tries to improve quality, the more he receives junk. And Tom isn't faring much better. Each man is getting more of the very thing he detests.

Claudia and Mandy tackled the problem of quality differently, but arrived at a similar impasse:

CLAUDIA: "My team leader, Mandy, can't be pleased. She thinks she has a better way to do everything, so she's always making me redo things. And such a temper! I've begun asking more questions, to make sure I'm going to do something exactly the way she wants it. But when I ask, she barks, 'Not that way! Here, let me do it.' Then she grabs the file out of my hand and I stand there feeling like an idiot. I'm afraid to do anything! The harder I try to do it her way, the more she treats me like a stupid little twit."

MANDY: "My new assistant, Claudia, drives me up the wall. She's so hesitant and tentative. Every sentence out of her mouth is a question, like 'Do you think we should do X now?' or 'Where do you want me to keep this file?' I was told she is smart, but you'd never know it. I may as well do everything myself."

The more careful and hesitant Claudia gets, the more Mandy yells at her. The more Mandy yells and grabs things away, the more hesitant Claudia becomes. Their interactions are like a well-rehearsed dance: Yell, hesitate—hesitate, yell, cha-cha-cha.

The curious thing in both of these examples is that each person's way of handling the other's annoying behavior ends up encouraging *more* of that behavior, not less. This is the predictable element in seemingly unchangeable situations: When you can't get someone to change, the way you are going about it is probably making things worse.

Once caught up in that dance, your situation may feel hopeless. But it's not. When you learn to recognize the steps of your particular dance, you can then learn how to change them. So before you fire that technician, yell at your friend, or quit your job, let me show you how to take the lead and change the dance. You have all the influence you need. You just have to learn how to use it.

You're More Influential Than You Think

When we can't get someone to change, we may say it is because Tom needs to throw his weight around or Mandy is an incurable perfectionist or Claudia lacks initiative. In other words, we say it's because of that person's character or personality. This traditional view presumes that problems reside *within* individuals, separate and distinct from the person's environment. It presumes that our actions don't influence others' behavior. Once a jerk, always a jerk, so to speak.

Of course people do have different personalities and habits—some annoying. That's not the issue. The issue is that you either reinforce or discourage Tom or Mandy or Claudia's habits by your own reactions. By looking at your own actions as well as theirs, you can learn to respond to their irritating manner in a way that extinguishes it instead of igniting it. It's like watching a chess game.

When we watch two people playing chess, there is no question that each person reacts to what the other person does. Player A moves a chess piece, setting the game in motion. Player B then makes a move that takes Player A's piece into account. This move then influences Player A's next move. The game advances in this fashion: The moves of one player influence and, in turn, are influenced by the moves of the other.

In a chess game the reciprocal influence is obvious. But when we are trying to get someone to change, we may not think about how our actions influence the other person's behavior. We think about how much their actions annoy us. Thus we take the traditional one-sided perspective. To see how this plays out, let's listen to Andy and Carolyn, who are struggling with Martha, their nitpicking manager. Here are their one-sided views of what's going on:

> ANDY: "I don't know what's wrong with me. I just can't seem to please Martha no matter what I do. I'm staying late most evenings just to try and get everything perfect, but I always miss something that she picks up on. I'm beginning to think I'll never learn this job."
>
> CAROLYN: "Martha is so inept. She gives me a new assignment and then leaves me without a clue about what she really wants or where to find the information I need. But she sure loves to nitpick when I'm done. She is so frustrating to work for!"

If this were a chess game, Andy would be watching only his pieces and the moves he's made, and would find it baffling that his pieces kept disappearing off the board. Carolyn, on the other hand, would watch only Martha's pieces, and would ignore how her own moves let Martha win. This would not be a very satisfying game of chess, and this is an equally unsatisfying way to look at a problem.

To deal effectively with Martha, Andy and Carolyn must not

focus on themselves or on Martha in isolation, but must refocus on what's going on between Martha and Andy and between Martha and Carolyn. It is possible that Martha is not a good manager, or that Andy doesn't know his job, or that Carolyn never asks enough questions about an assignment. However, one player can't arbitrarily decide she's won the chess game and declare checkmate. The other player must make moves that let her win. So to solve their problems with each other, the question is not what's wrong with Andy or with Carolyn or with Martha. The question is: What is each person doing that makes the other person act as he or she does and what do they need to do instead?

Seeing Both Sides

The Marthas of the world can make you feel miserable and help-less. It seems farfetched to think you influence them. But, in fact, you *do* actively influence them—unfortunately, to continue making you miserable. You're still playing chess. You're just losing the game.

In your defense, the person you're wishing to change may be a better player than you are. Let's say that your boss likes to explode when displeased—a move obviously designed to obliterate the opponent (you). It is not easy to come up with an effective countermove as your heart thumps, your mouth goes dry, and your career passes before your eyes. Your next move will probably revolve around trying to survive this explosion and avoid the next one. Your exploder boss then whispers, "Checkmate!"

But even with such a boss, you're still choosing your response. You may not know all the choices available, so you may choose ineffective ones, but you're always choosing. (Later in this book, you'll read about a creative and effective response to such an "exploder.") You have options no matter what's going on. On his radio show the comedian Jack Benny had a routine about a robber. Jack, notoriously stingy, is accosted by this fellow who hollers, "Your money or your life!" Silence follows. The robber finally yells, "Hey, I said your money or your life!" Jack Benny replies, "I'm thinking, I'm thinking! Don't rush me!"

Next Steps

Throughout this book you will meet clients of mine from a variety of businesses—from *Fortune* 500 organizations to small family concerns, from high-tech aerospace companies to manufacturing firms. (Their names and companies have been disguised to protect the innocent—and the guilty.) I know that many of their struggles will be familiar to you since I've heard these problems described frequently in my twenty-seven years of consulting. You will also read about people's struggles with their spouses, children, and friends. Even if you haven't endured a particular problem, its resolution may still give you ideas for the problem you do face. I suggest that, as you read, you keep in mind a particular person who bothers you. You will learn faster by applying this process as you go along.

To make this book both easy to read and to use as a reference, I have divided it into three sections. Section I of the book builds the foundation for successfully getting people to change. You will learn how to see people's difficult behavior in a new light and how to bring into clear focus what you need them to change. These chapters will show you how to save considerable time and effort.

Section II describes the five commonsensical ways people

try to get others to change—methods that rarely work but that everybody tries. You'll learn how to avoid these traps and what to do instead.

Section III walks you through the steps of applying all you've learned—ten ways to pick a successful strategy for your particular problem, how to troubleshoot your plan, and how to learn this process quickly.

Periodically you will find application exercises separated from the text by lines, as this paragraph is. You may want to pause and work on your current problem. For those of you who prefer to read the entire book before tackling your problem, I suggest skimming the application exercises for ideas rather than skipping them entirely.

TWO

Maddening Circles of Common Sense: How We Get in the Way of Change

Your manager takes credit for your ideas, your assistant avoids extra work at all costs, while another member of your staff spends too much time on low-priority tasks. You've tried over and over to get them to change, but to your increasing frustration, they don't. There's a good reason why they don't: You inadvertently told them not to. To see how such a thing can happen, we'll look in on Sheila, a thirty-six-year-old features editor in her fourth year at a weekly news magazine, who has just finished a meeting with her boss, Tom.

Sheila strides down the hall to her office, slams her door, and throws the manuscript on her desk. Another rotten meeting with her boss. Tom, her imperious managing editor, always makes her defensive. His tone of voice ("SURELY you didn't think THIS would be acceptable, DID you, hmmm?") had her stammering explanations within two seconds ("Well, I hadn't really finished it. I just wanted to see if you thought I was headed in the right direction"). She hated how Tom smirked while lecturing her on how to rewrite the article. She tried several times to explain that she'd already considered his ideas, but she knew she sounded defensive—again—and that he probably didn't believe her anyway. He always interrupted her with, "You're not listening." It happened every time! She stares at the file, hating him, furious at herself, and wishing she could quit.

No doubt Tom's actions were infuriating. But what Sheila didn't realize was that she had actually cued Tom to act that way. Let's take a closer look.

Maddening Circles: How We Help People Drive Us Crazy

The ways people can drive us crazy vary greatly, but how we help them do it rarely does. It's our efforts to get them to change that get us in trouble. Here are the two simple steps we take, all too often, that prolong rather than resolve our problems with others:

STEP ONE: WE ATTEMPT A REASONABLE SOLUTION THAT DOESN'T WORK.

To get someone to change, we do or say something that common sense says should work. When Tom tells Sheila that her writing needs more work, Sheila quickly explains her reasons for writing what she did. It's certainly a logical response. It just doesn't work. Tom interrupts her explanations and continues his lecture.

STEP TWO: WHEN THE PERSON DOESN'T CHANGE, WE CONTINUE DOING MORE OF THE SAME THING THAT ISN'T WORKING (FREQUENTLY IN AN EMBELLISHED MANNER).

Sheila continues to explain why she's rejected certain story angles. She again defends her choices, trying to get Tom to understand. The result: He lectures her again, telling her that she isn't listening. She then defends again and he lectures again.

Sheila had tried a reasonable solution that didn't happen to work. She didn't realize how her ineffective solution—repeated over and over—created this circular dance:

> the more Sheila gives explanations for her choices
>
> the more Tom lectures her on how to write

When I talked with Sheila, she was ready to quit. She believed that she'd tried her best to get through to Tom. She instead had taken the two steps that predictably make things worse. Sheila had dealt with Tom logically, all right. But when her efforts didn't change how he treated her, she didn't try a different approach. She did essentially what she had done before.

The "More-of-the-Same" Dance

With those two steps, we cue the very behavior we want others to change. The more we repeat our cue, the more they do what annoys us. If you've ever felt like you've been going around and around with someone, like Sheila and Tom, you probably have.

Everybody does it now and again. For example, Sally, vice

president of accounting for a Boston training company, used threats of demotion and termination to keep her people on their toes. She didn't realize that the resulting stress made many people perform worse, not better. When Sally noticed someone's performance slipping, she'd threaten them again. She didn't see the connection between her threats and their diminishing performance. Predictably (to everyone but Sally), her action exacerbated rather than solved problems. She created this more-of-the-same dance:

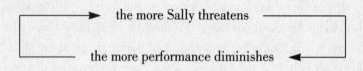

the more Sally threatens

the more performance diminishes

It's hard to believe that people continually repeat a "solution" that isn't working. But we all make this mistake now and again. We usually do it blindly and with the best of intentions (to get someone to stop driving us crazy). Often we vary our later efforts—we get louder, we send E-mail instead of meeting—but our basic approach remains the same. Unfortunately, when we use the same tactic over and over—embellished or not—we trigger rather than eliminate the very behavior we're trying to change.

But wait. We don't always mishandle troublesome behavior. When we are not getting results, we often rethink the situation, drop the ineffective solution, and find something else that works. End of difficulty. So if sometimes we switch strategy, why at other times do we stick with one that locks us into battle? There are several reasons. Let's start with the major one—the "story" we tell ourselves about our troubles.

A Closer Look: How We Blind Ourselves

When we first try to change someone's behavior, few of us take the time to analyze the situation and plan our strategy. We simply dive in. We may try something that worked for us in a similar situation. Usually we choose a solution that fits our normal style. For instance, when yelled at by a colleague, a shy or pensive individual may withdraw silently whereas an assertive or competitive person might reflexively say, "Hey, back off!"

If our first reaction gets our colleague to quit yelling at us, then we go on about our lives. If it doesn't, we tell ourselves a little story: "She yelled to make me look bad in front of my staff." Or, "She yelled at me because she's been under a lot of stress lately."

We do this to make sense of what's happening to us, yet we forget that it's just a little story we've told ourselves that may or may not be accurate. If our story is accurate and leads us to an effective solution, great. The mischief begins when we act as if our story is true—and it's not. For instance, your colleague has been yelling at you for three weeks and you assume that she is trying to make you look bad. But what if she is simply under tremendous stress and hasn't slept much this month? Because of your story, you may bop her on the nose with a rolled-up newspaper when, in fact, what she needs is sympathy. Your reaction, triggered by your story, will more than likely make the situation worse.

Our stories often mislead us. Unfortunately, not many of us like to admit that we may have misread a situation. We stick with our story in spite of evidence to the contrary. Or as Norman Maier, the author of numerous business psychology books, put it: "If the facts do not conform to your theory, they must be disposed of."

Forcing the Facts to Fit the Theory

We selectively choose the facts we weave into our stories. In the following situation two men end up in a protracted conflict fueled by their stories. The italicized phrases point out each man's spin on the facts. Jim, an experienced manager newly transferred to the business accounts department of a West Coast bank, had a problem with Paul, a talented employee now reporting to him. Here is what he said:

> JIM: I just took over this department two months ago and, while I've been in management a long time, I'm new to business accounts. When I came onboard, I told everyone I'd be looking over their shoulders until I got comfortable with business accounts and to please bear with me. Then I met with each person to go over workloads, responsibilities, and needs. All went well until I got to Paul. When I met with him, he sat there like a lump and I had to drag answers out of him. How am I supposed to make sure the department has all the resources it needs if I don't know what people are doing? The way he acts, *he must be up to something.* I was surprised too because he's been in the department for years, and I'd been told that he's one of the best in his field. Maybe he hasn't got enough to do and *is just coasting.* I'm not sure what he does all day, but he sure resents my asking him about it. *He's hiding something.* I'm sure of it. And I intend to find out what.

As the italicized words indicate, Jim has begun to create his story about Paul. Rather than keep an open mind, Jim picks one explanation for Paul's behavior and locks on to it. His story prompts him to demand more and more information from Paul.

Now let's see what the situation looked like from Paul's point of view:

> PAUL: This was the best job in the world until Jim came along. He *has to stick his nose in everything*. He wants to know every move you make, double-check every decision, review every piece of paper. What is this, kindergarten? The guy's *a real micromanager*. I've been in this job ten years and I've never had a problem. My performance reviews have always been just fine and I've often gotten bonuses for my work. I just do the best I can and mind my own business. The way he acts, you'd think I was a crook. You know, I think *he's looking for some way to blow me out of here and bring in his own people*.

New managers have been known to push employees out in order to bring in their own people, and there are managers who make the mistake of micromanaging. Paul could have been right about Jim. But he wasn't, and his story led him to withhold information from that "micromanager," which made Jim even more suspicious. Their stories led them to this more-of-the-same routine:

the more Paul withdraws and withholds information

the more Jim demands reviews and information

With every demand Jim makes, Paul has additional "proof" that his story is true. And as Paul clams up more, he "proves" that Jim has read him accurately.

When people reach this stage, it is hard for them to reconsider their stories about the situation, much less notice that those stories lead to actions that trigger the irritating behavior. As Michael Shermer, author of *Why People Believe Weird Things,* states, "It's the same sort of logic at work in conspiracy theories. I put it this way: I wouldn't have seen it if I hadn't believed it."

Once the more-of-the-same dance is firmly entrenched, it's impossible to change the other person's actions—that is, *if* you keep doing what you've been doing. But your story will indicate that what you've been doing is right, so as long as you cling to your story, you won't see that you need to do something different.

Everyone Is a Storyteller

It's natural to make up stories and everyone does it. But seeing events from only one perspective can (and usually does) lead to misinterpretation. Unfortunately, our story—our interpretation of the facts and of people's intentions—becomes truth to us, making it difficult to contemplate a different perspective. We often reinforce the "truth" by telling and retelling the story to friends and family. Think about how often you sit in the coffee room or at the dinner table talking about your frustration with someone. In most cases, you focus on how difficult (stupid, mean, selfish, cowardly) the other person is and how unfairly he treats you. With each telling the villain becomes more vile (and you more virtuous). You're sure that you've got him all figured out.

Such stories provide a certain comfort—that you're right, that the problem is not your fault, that you're doing the best you can in a difficult situation. Unfortunately, this one-sided view—concentrating on what's "wrong" with the other person—keeps you from noticing what *you* do that provokes your villain's behavior. Your story implies that you're doing the only reasonable thing and, as you repeat your "reasonable" solution, you reinforce rather than change the other person's annoying behavior. Your actions unintentionally say, "I hate it when you do X. Do it some more."

Chasing Your Own Tail: How We Become the Problem

With some problems, like procrastination or excessive worrying, we have only ourselves to deal with (although well-meaning friends may exacerbate the situation by offering the same ineffective advice we've been giving ourselves). But when we can't break our own bothersome habit, we can be sure that we picked, and continually repeated, an ineffective way to tackle that habit. And hidden in the woodwork of our minds will be the story that cues us to keep trying the same old thing. For example, everyone has trouble sleeping once in a while. Some people simply view this as a temporary discomfort; they drink warm milk and read until they're sleepy again. Other people try to force themselves back to sleep. Their story may go something like, "I've just got to get back to sleep; I'll be a wreck tomorrow if I don't. There must be something wrong with me; no one else has this much trouble. Oh why does this always happen to me?" The more they try to force sleep, which their story cues them to do, the more elusive sleep becomes. So whether your problem is with another person or with your own habits, your ineffective solution, repeated over and over, perpetuates your problem.

Justin, a distribution manager in an East Coast mail-order company, was feeling down. To cheer himself up, he recited all the reasons for feeling good about himself and his life (lovely wife, nice children, good-paying job, good career prospects), and tried to talk himself out of his mood. But this didn't work and he felt more depressed. He began to view each low moment as part of a growing trend and worried that he was becoming seriously depressed. As he focused only on the down times, he ignored the many times he felt normal, even good. His story (that he should feel happy, that he was feeling low more and more often) led him to interpret the normal ups and downs of life as the beginnings of a major depression. The more he told himself that he should feel chipper, the more severe and frequent his low moods appeared to him. But he was like a dog chasing its tail:

> the more he told himself he should be happy
>
> the more he felt depressed

His efforts to resolve his problem now perpetuated it, and his story told him to keep trying the same thing anyway.

Whether we're trying to change someone else's habits or our own, sometimes we all stick with a solution that doesn't work. We think it should work, so we keep trying—not realizing that this ineffective solution is now holding us back by perpetuating the behavior we are trying to change. And our stories—which led us to the ineffective solution in the first place—cue us to keep trying the same old unsuccessful thing.

Your Story

Maybe your story about that co-worker who is out to get you *is* 100 percent accurate (and insightful too, of course). But try to imagine a different explanation for your co-worker's behavior. Is she reacting to something you might innocently have done or said? Questioning your story isn't easy, but being at war with your co-worker isn't much fun either.

The following exercise will help you figure out your story. Think about a problem you're having with someone or a personal habit you'd like to change. If you don't have a current problem, skim the exercise or work through a past problem that didn't turn out well.

CHECKING OUT YOUR STORY

1. Write down the problem you're having with someone's troublesome behavior.

   EXAMPLES OF PROBLEMS
   Manager: "I have to solve all the problems for my project leaders. They show no initiative, even though they're the ones out on the shop floor every day. They just wait for me to figure out a solution. It wastes a lot of my time."
   Colleague: "My co-worker thinks she has all the answers. No matter what I'm talking about, she has to tell me how to deal with it. Her constant advice drives me crazy."
   Employee: "I just can't get myself to finish things on time. No matter what I promise myself, I always wait until the last minute. The stress is terrible, but I just can't seem to plan ahead."

2. Describe why you think the problem exists. This will be your "story" about the problem.

   EXAMPLES OF STORIES
   Manager: "Why won't my project leaders solve their own problems? Because they don't want to take responsibility.

They don't want to confront each other and deal with conflict. They'd rather let me tell people what to do."

Colleague: "Why does my co-worker give me all that advice? Because she thinks she knows everything. She was a teacher for years and thinks it's still her job to teach everyone. It's such a knee-jerk reaction that I don't think she could stop if she wanted to."

Employee: "Why don't I plan? I guess because I've always been a procrastinator. I do my best work when I'm under pressure. I'm not any good at planning; it's just not my thing."

3. Now translate this one-sided story into a two-sided view of the situation. Write down what you think the other person's story would be about your behavior. Rather than lamenting the troublesome behavior that you described in step one, treat it as if it were the sensible response to what *you* are doing or saying.

EXAMPLES

Manager: "I'll bet they'd say that I don't listen very well, that I jump in and tell them what to do. In fact, one project leader accused me of being afraid to let them handle problems. They'd say I'm too quick to take over."

Colleague: "My co-worker would probably say that I worry about a problem incessantly, but never do anything about it. She'd think that all I do is fret."

When working on your own habits:
To find the other side of your story (that might lead to a better solution), ask yourself: What are the benefits of this problem that I might lose if I resolved it?

EXAMPLE

Employee: "Well, I can work late and avoid the hassles at home. It also looks good to my manager to log a lot of hours. I'd lose those advantages if I stopped procrastinating."

You now have a snapshot of your one-sided story. You also have a view from the other side—what you may be doing that inadvertently perpetuates your problem. When you can't get someone to change, check out your story. It is probably limiting your thinking to the it's-their-fault viewpoint, which won't help you solve your problem.

Repeating the Solution: How Do We Get Caught?

Our story is the major reason we try the same ineffective solution over and over. Three other reasons can also keep us on the loop road to nowhere.

- WE GET CAUGHT IN THE WEB OF OUR
  OWN LOGIC.

When we're faced with a problem we've handled before, it's logical to try what worked the last time. When we're faced with a new problem, it's logical to try whatever seems the reasonable approach. If our efforts succeed, the problem is resolved. The trouble can occur if the solution doesn't happen to work. Sometimes we'll then reassess our approach and try a different one. At other times it doesn't occur to us to question our solution. We assume our solution should work and therefore it must have failed because we haven't applied it often enough, or firmly enough, or loudly enough. We get caught in the web of our logic—that since it's the "right" solution and therefore should work, we must keep trying it. As Fisch, Weakland, and Segal stated in *The Tactics of Change,* "Contrary to the widespread view that people are illogical, we propose that people are *too* logical; that is, they act logically in terms of basic, unquestioned premises, and when undesired results occur, they employ further logical operations to explain away the discrepancy, rather than revising the premises." So when a solution doesn't work, we don't stop to question whether it's the right solution, we just keep trying it. Repeating an ineffective solution is like talking louder and louder in English to a Parisian cabdriver. No matter how loudly you speak, he won't understand you.

"If at first you don't succeed, try, try again." This saying urges us to persevere. But "try, try again" doesn't necessarily mean to try the same thing again. If a solution doesn't work, repeating it won't work either. But it's hard to stop yourself because the solution seems so sensible. It was his logic that trapped Jim, the new manager at loggerheads with Paul. Jim's request for information had succeeded with his other employees, so it "should" have worked with Paul. Therefore it seemed logical to Jim to continue demanding information and reviews when his initial efforts didn't work. Logical, yes; effective, no.

So sometimes logic can be the culprit. Other times, we just don't realize what we are doing.

- WE DON'T REALIZE THAT WE ARE DOING THE
  SAME THING OVER AND OVER.

A second reason we don't change tactics is that we believe we already have. Judy, a frustrated manager in a Pittsburgh auto parts business, struggled to get Rob, her warehouse supervisor, to change. While talented and loyal, he often ignored his staff's suggestions and demanded they do things his way. Two good employees had transferred out of his unit in disgust.

Judy wanted Rob to listen to his workers' ideas. She said, "I don't know how many times I've talked with Rob about how he undercuts morale. I've told him how important it is to let the workers have a say, that his people have good ideas about how to improve things around here. I've told him how important it is for his career to listen to his employees. I've written the goal into his performance appraisal and reminded him at each of our one-on-one meetings. I sent him to a review course on listening skills. I've tried everything. Nothing gets through to him."

Although Judy genuinely believed she had tried everything, she had actually tried only one thing. Judy's one solution had been to tell Rob—face-to-face, in writing, in meetings, and at various decibel levels—that he should listen to his employees. Sending him to training was one more way of saying "Listen to your staff," this time hoping a trainer's words would finally get through to him. Because Judy didn't realize her efforts were all basically the same, it didn't occur to her to try something new. She thought she already had.

Like Judy, you may not see that you're doing the same thing over and over and can probably list an assortment of solutions you've tried. But a single theme will run through those solutions, and once you spot it, you can break free and try something new.

So sometimes we repeat a solution because we don't realize we're doing it. But at times we do know and repeat it anyway.

- WE CAN'T THINK OF ANYTHING BETTER
  TO TRY.

Sometimes we're fully aware that our efforts are useless, but having no idea what else to do, we try them again anyway. How many parents have you overheard say to their kids, "If I've told you once, I've told you a thousand times. . . !" And then they go for 1,001.

And people don't just do this with their kids. One business executive, talking about a talented but difficult engineer, said: "I've told him to change his behavior until I'm blue in the face. I know it doesn't do any good, but what else am I going to do? I can't fire him. He's the best in the business." The executive actually had many other options, but he saw only two—one ineffective and the other unacceptable.

So we repeat unproductive solutions for several reasons. In addition to creating a "story" that limits our solutions, we trap ourselves with logic ("This solution should work"); we don't realize that we are repeating the same solution; and we believe that no other option is possible. Any of these can keep us from trying something new.

Of course, not wanting to believe that we are in any way to blame for the problem also gets in the way. Not many of us want to look at our own behavior. We'd rather say that it's that other guy who caused the problem, and if he weren't so stubborn (lazy, self-serving) this problem would have been resolved long ago.

Unfortunately, pleading "Not guilty" doesn't get your problem fixed. There's only one way to get it fixed: Resist that seductive more-of-the-same solution, do something significantly different, and then watch your difficult person change.

> To change someone's problem behavior, change your solution.

Breaking the Maddening Circle

To finally get someone's annoying behavior to change, you need to stop using your "more-of-the-same" solution and find a new strategy. This three-question formula leads you to that new strategy.

1. WHAT IS THE PRIMARY PROBLEM?

Answering this question is not as easy as it may initially appear. People often think in generalities, as in "My husband is selfish." But generalities obscure the problem. He's probably not selfish about everything all the time. You'll need to know when he acts selfishly and about what, and what problem his selfishness creates.

You can't transform people, but you can get them to change specific troublesome behaviors. When you identify the particular trait that is bothersome, and the problem it produces, you're well on your way to changing it.

2. WHAT HAVE YOU BEEN DOING ABOUT YOUR PROBLEM SO FAR?

Identifying your more-of-the-same solution takes some practice initially. That one solution can disguise itself in more costumes than a Barbie doll. So until you figure out the identity of your favorite solution, the one your logic draws you to, you will continue to dress it up and trot it out.

3. WHAT DO YOU NEED TO DO INSTEAD?

Once you know specifically what you're trying to change, and what, specifically, doesn't work, then you can figure out what to do instead. Sometimes your new strategy will be straightforward. More often it will require a little fancy footwork. After all, you now have to handle both the original problem and the resistance you've created. You have to undo what your ineffective solution did.

You're about to attack your problem with a brand-new set of weapons. You'll start by answering the question "What's the primary problem?"

THREE

Just the Facts, Ma'am: Focusing on the Heart of the Matter

Figuring out specifically what you want someone to change seems like such a simple task. Your colleague (or boss or spouse) is driving you batty and should stop doing it. Not much to figure out, right? But if you're having trouble getting your colleague to stop doing it, the chances are that you haven't defined the "it." And if you are not clear about what you want changed, you can bet that your colleague isn't staying awake nights figuring it out for you.

When no one is clear about what is supposed to change, nothing does. And as your frustration grows about your colleague's annoying habit, you begin to think that a personality transplant is the only possible solution.

A typical example is Ted, a talented plant manager for a South Dakota window manufacturer. See if you can figure out what Ted is trying to get his peer Harry to change:

LUCY: "I understand there's a conflict between you and Harry."

TED: "Well, yes. The guy's really got an attitude—all hung up on being top gun. He wants control of everything."

LUCY: "What do you mean? What's Harry doing that's causing you a problem?"

TED: "Harry's just one of those people who—well, you know, 'old school.' Control the data and you control the world. He'll never let go."

LUCY: "It's clear that Harry is not your favorite person, but I'm not clear on what Harry is actually doing that's causing you a problem."

TED: "Well, I'm trying to tell you. You know he worked in corporate before coming into the field, so he's been trained to be a corporate guy. But his way just doesn't work out here, not when we're trying to empower people and all. But with his personality, I don't think he can change. It's hopeless."

LUCY: "*What* is hopeless? What does Harry do or say that you are wishing you could get him to change? What does he do that creates such a conflict? Would you describe the actual problem for me—what he says or does that bothers you so much?"

TED: "He just makes me so mad. He loves to tick people off, but I won't let him have the satisfaction of knowing I'm fuming. He ought to be fired, or at least sent back to corporate, but, for some reason, the boss likes him. I think it's because they're so much alike, both from the East Coast and all. The politics around here are really tricky."

LUCY: "But what's the problem?!"

Could you figure out what Ted's real problem with Harry was? I obviously couldn't. Ted truly believed he was describing his problem with Harry, but instead he labeled Harry ("old school, top gun"), speculated about why Harry does whatever he does ("wants control of everything, has an attitude"), stated what he thinks should happen to Harry ("be fired or sent back to corporate"), and took a shot at office politics to boot. He described everything except the central issue—what behavior Ted specifically wanted Harry to change. Maybe Harry ignores Ted's phone calls, or is late to staff meetings, or demands too much documentation, or steals his parking place. Until Ted defines what specifically causes him a problem with Harry, he doesn't stand a chance of figuring out how to get Harry to change.

Dragging In the Kitchen Sink, Too

Have you ever noticed that, when you're upset with someone, that person can do no right? All his little habits—slurping his coffee, chewing his thumbnail, doodling at meetings—suddenly become unbearable. But when the crisis is past and the aggravating issue is resolved, his slurping, chewing, and doodling seem insignificant. You remember the other things that you like or respect about him.

When we "drag in the kitchen sink," we're building a case against someone. Maybe we can feel blameless about the conflict if we see the other person as the villain (which a long list of flaws implies). But this doesn't help us clarify what we want to change. Instead, we work ourselves into a froth, blow the situation out of proportion, and consequently make it more difficult to figure out what the problem really is.

To succeed at getting someone to change, you have to first figure out what you want changed. Mumbling things like "He should be more professional" or "She should stop being such a jerk" just won't do it. For starters, what does "more professional" mean? What special brand of "jerk" is she? You have to get more specific. Start by sifting through your thoughts and feelings to identify the key elements—who, what, to whom, and how:

Who is doing
    what that presents a problem,
        to whom, and
            how is this behavior a problem?

Easy enough question. Unfortunately, the human mind is a complex machine, which makes thinking this simply a difficult task. But by the end of this chapter you will be able to program that two-eared computer of yours to spit out the facts you need. These facts make it possible to get people to change their irksome behavior.

Note that each component of the question asks for behaviors and facts, not interpretations of behaviors or judgments. Imagine a football coach reviewing a lost football game in Ted's vague manner. "Well, you guys played like a bunch of pansies. I've seen better moves from my grandmother." This won't help win the next game. Maybe a coach says such things, but he wouldn't stop there. He'd pull out the videotapes and figure out what caused the bungled plays. He'd figure out who needs to do what differently in the next game. In other words, you need to know what is actually happening—not indulge in judgments and speculations.

Now let's take this seemingly simple question apart. Determining the *who, what, to whom,* and *how* answers the first question of the process: "What is the primary problem?" This is how you identify exactly what behavior you need someone to change. Once that target is clear, figuring out the right approach will become obvious.

Plucking Out the Facts

In any attempt to change someone's behavior, it's crucial to focus on the facts of your situation. You'll need to become like Sergeant Joe Friday of the old *Dragnet* series. When crime scene witnesses rambled off into speculations or hearsay, he'd say, "Just the facts, ma'am."

Describing "Just the facts, ma'am" isn't always easy. When you've been frustrated for a while, your story comes to mind much faster than objective facts. Asked for "who is doing what," your mind dashes off like an unleashed puppy and drags back speculations about *why* the problem persists. Asked for "how the behavior is a problem," your thoughts wander off in various directions: justifying and judging and blaming, fussing and fuming, dwelling on anger or frustration or fear, and fretting about how hopeless things are, or you are, or they are.

You can't stop your mind from wandering, and you may be emotional about the situation. Most people start with a jumble of thoughts and feelings, especially when they have been frustrated for a while. But you can't change the situation without seeing the facts clearly, so here are the tools for rooting out those facts, even when your feelings are running rampant. Watch how Katherine, a regional sales manager for a large paper company, moves from frustrated to focused by carefully defining her problem.

PART ONE OF THE DEFINITION: *WHO*

KATHERINE: "I'm so distracted I can't work. I mean, everything's a mess. I hate my job. I fight with my husband.

I'm depressed and stressed all the time. I can't stand my
boss. I don't know what to do." And under her breath she
added, "And I feel fat!"

LUCY: "You mentioned a number of things that are
troubling you—your job, your husband, your boss, feeling
down. Which of these bothers you the most?"

KATHERINE: "I hate fighting with my husband, but it's
usually about what I should do about my boss, who's driving
me crazy. So I guess that my boss is my main problem. If I
could do something about him, I don't think I'd feel so depressed. If I wasn't so depressed, I probably wouldn't fight
with my husband so much."

In your own situation you may be quite clear about who is
the problem and can therefore answer this part of the definition
as quickly as Katherine. But when your problem persists, many
parts of your life may be affected and the actual problem can get
lost in the shuffle. Usually, though, one key issue is causing your
distress. Even if several problems concern you, one thing is certain: You can't fix them all at once. So picking your most troublesome problem is the critical first step.

Katherine has defined the **who**—an important first step.
Now she needs to figure out what, exactly, her boss does that
causes the problem.

PART TWO OF THE DEFINITION:
WHO IS DOING *WHAT*?

LUCY: "So it sounds like your boss is the place to start.
What problem are you having with him?"

KATHERINE: "Everything! He doesn't care about anything but his own career. He's rude, uncaring, and abrupt. He ignores me and never gives me any encouragement. He answers the phone when I'm trying to talk with him; he cancels appointments at the very last minute even if I've told him it's important that I meet with him. Recently he gave me a new assignment—a high-profile project, I might add—and promptly left town for two weeks. I have no idea if I'm on the right track with this assignment, and I can't get his attention long enough to find out. Like I said, he just doesn't care. And just try to get a compliment out of him! I think his tongue would spasm if he said anything nice."

LUCY: "You've mentioned several things about your boss that are bothering you; mainly, though, that he's not giving compliments and not helping you with this new assignment. Which is the bigger problem, the one that bothers you the most?"

KATHERINE: "Well, this new assignment is really getting to me. I just have to get more guidance on what I'm supposed to do or I'll fail. This is a high-profile project, and I'm nervous. He's like this with all the assignments he doles out. Never gives any direction. I don't know where to begin, I don't know what's required, and he's never available to talk to. When I catch him in the hall, he always agrees to meet later. But 'later' never happens. Or he gives me five minutes, then tells me I should be able to figure out the assignment for myself. Sink or swim."

So Katherine's primary problem boils down to a lack of guidance from her manager, especially on a high-profile project. People often have a laundry list of issues that bug them about someone, but one particular item will usually be the real culprit. When that gets fixed, the relief is enormous. Taking the time to figure out your main beef is critical.

PART THREE OF THE DEFINITION:
WHO IS DOING WHAT *TO WHOM?*

In this case, the "to whom" is Katherine, since her manager is withholding guidance from her specifically. In most cases, the "to whom" will be you since you're the one struggling with the problem. But asking this question can be useful. You may discover that you've allowed others to dump their problems on you. If you ask, "To whom is this a problem?," and your answer is your office manager or your sister-in-law, for example, then you may find that your best strategy is to help them solve their own problem rather than letting them unload it on you. Or maybe you're working on a troublesome habit of your own and, by answering this question, find that you don't actually mind your habit—it's your spouse "to whom" your habit is a problem. Recognizing this can help you figure out your problem, which, in this case, is not the habit itself. Your actual problem is your spouse's nagging about your habit.

PART FOUR OF THE DEFINITION:
HOW IS THIS BEHAVIOR A PROBLEM?

LUCY: "So, Katherine, your main concern is that you're not getting the help you want from your boss on this new assignment. This may sound like an odd question, but how is this a problem for you?"

KATHERINE: "I have to present my final report to the new senior vice president and I don't know what she's expecting. There are a number of avenues I could take. I don't really understand the purpose of the study, so I could easily go off in the wrong direction and end up looking really stupid."

Katherine now knows specifically what to work on. Here's a closer look.

The Bare Bones

By answering the four questions, Katherine whittled her pile of problems down like this:

1. She started with a jumble of thoughts and feelings and issues:

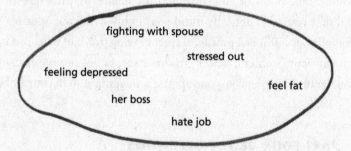

2. Katherine closed in on the key problem, in a general way:

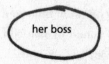

3. She found a jumble of thoughts and feelings about the problem with her boss:

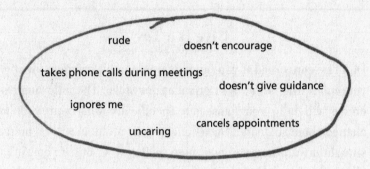

rude

doesn't encourage

takes phone calls during meetings

doesn't give guidance

ignores me

cancels appointments

uncaring

4. She figured out her primary complaint and the problem definition boiled down to:

- *Who:* her boss
- *is doing what:* not giving adequate guidance on projects
- *to whom:* Katherine
- *how this behavior is a problem:* Katherine is not sure how to proceed with her project and is worried about making sizable and highly visible mistakes.

In the beginning Katherine felt hopeless about a lot of things— her job, husband, boss, mood, and weight. Maybe you recognize the feeling. It happens when you lose track of what is specifically bothering you. Soon everything is bothering you. Too often you then rush around trying to fix the wrong thing. You go home and holler at your spouse for not balancing the checkbook. This not only doesn't fix your boss, you now have an angry spouse to contend with. (And this doesn't get the checkbook balanced either.) So before you make things worse, sit down and figure out what's really bugging you. By questioning your judgments, speculations, and stories you'll uncover the facts.

Give It a Try

Don't be concerned if you bumble around a bit trying to identify your main frustration. It's normal at this stage. The following exercise will help you figure out specifically what you want to change about someone. Occasionally your problem will be pretty straightforward and you can jump to step five. But if you are at all unclear about the problem, or you have several of them, then go through all the steps below. It will save you a lot of time and energy later.

FIGURING OUT "WHAT'S THE PROBLEM?"

Continue with the problem you began exploring on page 38. You can use Katherine's problem search on page 54 as an illustration.

1. List all the issues that are bothering you. At this stage, let yourself ramble. Some people prefer writing a list. Others find it helpful to talk into a tape recorder and then list issues from the replay.
2. Since you can't effectively work on all problems at once, decide which area or particular person bothers you the most. Don't be surprised if you go back and forth a little, but pick the one that, if you fixed it first, would bring you the most relief. Circle that issue or person's name on your list.

3. Focus on what you circled. It is probably somewhat general at this stage, so list all the things that bother you about this issue or person. (Katherine, at this point, had only identified her boss as the main difficulty. She needed to figure out what in particular about him was causing the distress.)

4. Now pick the key problem to work on. Which of the items you listed in step three bothers you the most? Which one, if you fixed it first, would get you the most mileage? You may vacillate at first, as Katherine did, but look for what's most troublesome to you. If you're having trouble choosing, ask yourself: If you could fix only one item on your list and had to live with all the others, what would you choose?

5. Now focus on that particular problem and spell out specifically:

> **Who** is doing
> > **what** that presents a problem,
> > > **to whom,** and
> > > > **how** is this behavior a problem?

Occasionally, just determining what the primary problem is helps you discover why you can't get someone to change: You've been working on the wrong problem. For example, Jerry, a young and gifted programmer for a Silicon Valley computer firm, couldn't get his uncommunicative boss to be open and friendly. He would drop by her office and ask about her weekend. "Fine," his boss would reply. End of topic. Jerry would start their meetings with small talk but his boss would abruptly interrupt to ask about a deadline.

When Jerry finally defined his problem, it turned out to be:

- **Who:** Jerry's boss
- *is doing **what:*** often neglecting to relate information from executive planning meetings that could affect current projects
- **to whom:** to Jerry and his team
- **how** *this behavior is a problem:* Jerry and his team miss opportunities to lobby for projects; they waste time on projects that will be canceled.

Jerry had tried to transform this woman's personality, thinking a talkative boss would disclose more information. But his manager's personality wasn't the problem; lack of information was. Jerry's solution had actually been annoying to his boss, a private person of few words. So the boss had been avoiding him because Jerry seemed a chatty time waster. Jerry had inadvertently found a way to get even less information by setting up this more-of-the-same cycle:

```
    ┌──────► the more Jerry tries to engage in small talk ──────┐
    │                                                            │
    └─ the more his boss avoids him, communicating even less ◄───┘
```

Jerry quit the small talk and instead directly asked for information on particular projects. He got what he needed. As a bonus, Jerry's boss stopped avoiding him and their working relationship improved.

It Doesn't Take Two to Tangle

What if it's your own habits that drive you crazy, like indecisiveness, fear of giving speeches, overeating? To figure out what to do, you still answer the same question: "Who is doing what, to whom, and how is it a problem?" For example, John, a sales representative for a farm equipment company in Kansas, had been offered a regional sales position but was vacillating about taking the important promotion. In the new position he would have to make presentations to large groups several times a year, and John was worried that his occasional stuttering would set him up for ridicule. He began to pay more attention to his stuttering and to worry that it was increasing. But when he defined his problem, he saw a different picture:

- *Who:* John Harrington
- *is doing what:* feeling afraid of increased stuttering
- *to whom this is a problem:* to himself
- *how this is a problem:* His concern about others' reactions if he should stutter during a presentation was leading him to turn down a promotion.

John then saw that he feared a *potential* increase in his stuttering. He realized that there was no actual problem yet and he reminded himself that he already knew several ways to cope with his occasional difficulty. He began to relax about the promotion.

Next Steps

Now let's troubleshoot your definition and make sure you focused on the facts of the situation and didn't get sidetracked by speculations or emotions.

FOUR

Tackling the Right Problem: Avoiding Bogs and Dead Ends

Clearly defining your primary problem will save you much wasted effort, even though searching for that definition can seem like searching for treasure in a maze. But now you have instructions that will show you the way through the maze and they read: To find the treasure, answer "Who does what to whom and how is this behavior a problem?"

So off you go to answer "Who is doing what?" and suddenly find yourself knee-deep in whys and wherefores ("I know why she's doing X—she's such a . . . !"). You regroup, study the instructions, and trudge bravely onward to answer "How is her behavior a problem?" But soon you're off course again, wading through speculations about what she's up to and how to get even. And because these paths seem familiar to you, you may not notice you're lost. What you notice instead is a growing conviction that your problem is hopeless: a dead giveaway that you took a wrong turn.

Let's look more closely at the two most tempting wrong turns in this maze. The first one will bog you down in "whys." The second will unceremoniously abandon you at a dead end.

THE FIRST DETOUR: THIS WAY TO THE BOG

The first detour is frequently traveled and therefore all the more inviting. To take this detour, simply speculate about *why* someone is troublesome rather than describing who is doing the troublesome behavior and what precisely he is doing. There are four ways to get yourself bogged down in "whys," and each is guaranteed to confuse you with superfluous issues and worries. You can: 1) focus on possible reasons for someone's behavior, 2) speculate about what people are up to, 3) label behavior instead of describing it, or 4) worry about who's right or wrong. Let's take them one at a time.

THE FIRST MISTAKE: "I KNOW WHY YOU'RE DOING THIS!"

"The problem is that this is a male-dominated organization," said Karen, a project leader in an Oregon manufacturing concern. Although Karen is convinced this is her real problem, she hasn't actually described her problem at all. Instead she has raised a possible reason for her problem. She's alleging that the male dominance in the organization is why she has some as-yet-unnamed problem. Continuing in this direction quickly bogged her down. Thinking that she'd defined her problem, Karen focused on the troubles inherent in "a male-dominated organization." The more she thought about how males dominate and females get ignored, how deeply entrenched such behavior must be, and how hard therefore to get taken seriously, the more depressed she became. "The problem is hopeless," she lamented. "This organization will never change." And while she dreaded searching for a new job, she could see no other solution.

Karen's mistake is a common one. When someone's driving you batty, it's normal to groan and think, "Why is he doing this to me!" Then you're off into the land of whys. That's why sticking to the formula of "Who does what to whom and how is this a problem?" is so important. Without the answer to that question, you can count on getting bogged down in issues that blow your problem out of proportion, like Karen did. Since Karen wasn't working on her actual problem, she couldn't figure out how to solve it and the more she thrashed around (as anyone who remembers old Tarzan movies knows), the farther she sank in the bog. When she finally stopped and described the specific behavior that was causing her distress, she was surprised. The "who" turned out to be two men—not the entire organization. The "what" turned out to be these two men routinely ignoring her requests for information. By describing the problem instead of reasons for the problem, she whittled her seemingly hopeless situation down to a manageable size.

It's not easy to avoid this bog. Your speculation about why a problem exists can sound like a plausible description of it. Suppose you describe your troubles with your manager by saying, "She's a new manager and insecure." This sounds like a problem description, but it only indicates your belief that *because* she is new and insecure, you are having some problem with her. It doesn't describe what troublesome things your manager is doing or saying that have become a problem for you. Keep going down this road and you'll end up trying to fix your manager's insecurity (that may not have anything to do with what's bothering you). But, if you stick to behaviors, such as "She doesn't give clear directions when giving out assignments," you will have a concrete problem to work on and a much better chance of finding a way to change her behavior. After all, a manager can learn how to give directions even if she happens to be new and insecure.

So sometimes you will get offtrack by speculating on general reasons for your problem's existence instead of actually defining the problem, as in the examples above. At other times, you'll make the second mistake: attributing your problem to someone's sinister or selfish motives.

THE SECOND MISTAKE: "I KNOW WHAT YOU'RE UP TO!"

The second way to get bogged down is to speculate about people's intentions instead of describing what they do that bothers you.

- "He only cares about his own career."
- "She's trying to make me look bad."
- "She's just playing this for sympathy."
- "He's maneuvering to get that plum assignment."

Such speculations only rile you up and make it harder for you to see the situation clearly. Occasionally you will guess correctly about someone's intentions. But usually you'll be wrong, and often quite wrong. Years of consulting have shown me that people are usually convinced they know what the other person is up to, but they are rarely right.

No one can know for sure what motive drives another person. (It's hard enough sometimes to figure out our own motives.) Your speculations will only obscure other possible explanations for their actions, and worse yet, will complicate rather than clarify your situation.

Nancy, a department head for a New Jersey telecommunications enterprise, fell into this trap. Frustrated with Maureen, another department head who often didn't inform her of plan changes, Nancy began to speculate that Maureen was out to get her. Any time Maureen didn't inform her of a change, Nancy saw it as further proof of malice. There was no possibility (in her mind) that Maureen didn't realize the impact some change might have on Nancy's department or that, in the midst of a hectic day, Maureen simply forgot to inform her.

When you're busy speculating about what someone is up to, you stop seeing *who* is doing *what*—the information you need. You may miss an easy fix for your problem. Since Nancy was convinced of Maureen's ill will, it never occurred to her to try the obvious: Tell Maureen the impact of her sudden changes and let her know what changes Nancy needed to hear about immediately. It took a blowup to bring the truth to light—that Maureen was oblivious to the havoc her changes caused in Nancy's department. Once she knew, she made a point of keeping Nancy informed.

You can't observe intentions, so you can never know for sure why someone acts a certain way. But you can observe actions and so can know for sure *what* someone is *saying* or *doing* that is causing you distress. That information will help you get them to quit it.

THE THIRD MISTAKE: "I KNOW WHAT YOU ARE!"

"He's rude . . . uncaring," said Katherine of her boss. While she thought she was describing his behavior, Katherine had fallen into the trap of using *label*s, which are merely vague explanations for behavior. Katherine was actually saying that because he's "rude and uncaring," her boss does whatever annoying thing he does. Perhaps he ignores her in meetings or tells off-color jokes or leaves the coffeepot empty. Her labels don't clarify what she wants him to change. So she is no closer to a solution. In fact, she is farther away from solving the problem because labeling behavior creates two problems.

First, labels are inherently vague and so they blur your view of the problem. While they leave you with the impression that you have defined the problem ("He's rude"), they don't describe the specific behaviors you need to work on—what he actually does or says that you have labeled rude. So you don't have the facts you need to resolve the problem. Second, labels imply someone simply IS a certain way and therefore unchangeable. So labels often make the situation appear more difficult, if not impossible, to change. For instance, the label "uncaring" may raise the specter of a cold and hard-to-reach person, which makes it easier to feel hopeless about changing such a person. Such labels bog down your thinking.

Describing the behaviors that the labels represent usually cuts the problem back down to size. When Katherine, whose boss never gave her guidance on assignments, translated "rude" into the specific behaviors that bothered her, "rude" became "answers the phone during meetings and cancels appointments." That behavior, while unpleasant, can certainly be changed, whereas the label "rude" simply writes the man off. Her label of "uncaring" boiled down to "doesn't give compliments." A person can be quite caring but not in the habit of giving compliments. Her boss's answering the phone in meetings and not giving compliments are resolvable problems. Stripped of her labels, Katherine's problem became much simpler to handle. As a matter of fact, neither of these issues turned out to be her main concern. In the end she didn't need to deal with them at all.

THE FOURTH MISTAKE: "I KNOW WHO'S RIGHT!"

Beware of one more common mistake that will trip you up: thinking in terms of right and wrong. Dwelling on who's right (you, of course) and who's wrong (the other person, naturally) brings you no closer to a definition of your problem. When you classify yourself as right, you're less likely to wonder about your contribution to the problem. Your friends will nudge you down this side road by commiserating with you, pointing out how wronged you are and what an idiot the other person is. While soothing to the ego, it doesn't show you how to get that "idiot" to change. To get someone to change, you need information, not solace. You need to return to "Just the facts, ma'am."

When you conjure up reasons, speculate about intentions, label, or take sides, you march yourself into a bog of whys. These four mistakes are simply different forms of explaining a possible *why* rather than describing the actual *what*. They don't help you get anyone to change. Just like Karen and her "male-dominated organization," *why* magnifies your problem and usually ties you up in knots.

> To get people to change their behavior, you need to know **what** is happening: who did what, not why they did it.

With the following exercise you can double-check that you're on the right track and that your definition will get you out of the maze.

TROUBLESHOOTING YOUR DEFINITION

Look back at the problem statement you sketched out in the previous application exercise on page 56:

1. Translate any labels ("unsure," "lazy," "micromanages," "political animal") into the behaviors these labels represent by asking yourself: What does the person do or say that leads me to pick that label?
2. Translate any speculations you've made about someone's motives or intentions into clear-cut behaviors by asking yourself: What specifically is the person doing or saying that led to my speculation about her motives?
3. Now take your answers from steps one and two and apply the videotape test: Is there anything in your answers that would not show up on a videotape recording of that person in action? ("Rude behavior" wouldn't play across the screen, but someone interrupting you to answer a phone would.) Rewrite any descriptions on your list that fail the test.

THE SECOND DETOUR:
ABANDONED AT A DEAD END

Even if you've avoided bogging yourself down in "whys," and have a clear grasp of who should change what, you're not out of the maze yet. You can still get off course at the second major detour. Many people do so by forgetting to answer *how* something is a problem or by jumping to solutions without bothering to define their situation at all. They usually end up wasting their time on the wrong problem. Let's look at these one at a time.

THE FIRST PATH TO THE DEAD END:

FORGETTING THE "HOW"

Some problems appear to be so obvious that you don't bother to figure out *how* someone's troublesome behavior is a problem. This makes it all too easy to wander off and work on the wrong problem. You can fall into this trap, for example, when you're frustrated with someone who doesn't do things your way. For instance, your assistant has a sloppy office, piles of papers covering her desk, table, and most of the floor. She knows where everything is and works well in the disarray, but you wouldn't be able to concentrate in such a mess. Your office is tidy, with only the current file centered neatly on your desk.

The more you see her messy work area, the more you become convinced that she couldn't possibly be productive surrounded by all that clutter. You begin to worry that she might lose some important paper. So you try to get her to clean it up. But she never gets around to it, citing her workload. Your irritation grows. You are sure she is less efficient than she could be. After all, you would be if you were working in such clutter. But, in fact, she gets her work done on time and never loses anything, not any more than you do, anyway.

So what is the problem you are solving? *How* is her messy desk a problem (if it is)? Is it, for example, that you can't find things when she is out of town? That certain important files rotating through the office get delayed at her desk? That your manager chides you about office tidiness? That you just don't like looking at the mess? When you haven't defined how a situation is a problem, you may end up attacking a problem that doesn't exist. But your efforts can bruise your relationship with the poor person you have decided to reform.

I remember watching Harold, a hyperactive supervisor with the Social Security Administration, nitpick Bess, a claims representative. Bess was quiet and efficient, but moved slowly, sauntering through the office as if living in the heat of the tropics. Harold, on the other hand, trotted across a room as if barefoot on hot sand. They approached everything at their own effective but distinct paces. Harold confused style with efficiency and kept trying to improve Bess even though she was one of the best in the office at processing claims promptly. But Harold didn't seem to no-tice that. After all, how could she be efficient when she moved so slowly! He never asked himself how her pace was a problem. The only progress Harold made was to completely antagonize Bess.

Always ask yourself how someone's behavior is a problem. The answer may save you a good deal of grief. To make sure you've covered this in your definition, take a moment to go through this exercise.

THE *HOW* OF YOUR PROBLEM

Defining how someone's behavior is a problem ensures that you are working on the right problem. To define the *how:*

1. Return to the problem statement you have been working on. Review the troublesome things people are doing and saying that you wrote down.
2. Then ask yourself: What actual problem does it create that he or she acts this way? *How* is this behavior a problem? You may go through a couple of iterations of this, as in: How is your assistant's messy desk a problem? Answer:

You can't find files on her desk when she's out of town. How is not being able to find files when she's gone a problem? Answer: Several times, not finding the files, you couldn't respond quickly to customers' queries and they got annoyed. OK. Now you can work on the resolvable problem of ready access to customers' files rather than on the nebulous problem of a messy desk.

There's one more path to avoid if you want to get someone to change. Let's take a look at it.

THE SECOND PATH TO THE DEAD END:

JUMPING TO THE SOLUTION

At times you will leap to a solution after just a cursory pass at defining the problem. You may believe that the problem is so obvious that you don't need to define it. For instance, Ted, who rambled on about his troubles with his peer Harry at the start of the last chapter, jumped to the half-baked conclusion that "Harry should be fired, or at least sent back to corporate." While Ted may relish that solution to his problem, it doesn't get him any closer to changing Harry's annoying behavior.

Sometimes your solution will hit the mark and resolve the problem. But if it didn't, and you are still coping with someone's annoying behavior, you need to back up and define the specifics—the who, what, to whom, and how—of your problem more carefully. Otherwise, the risk is too great of blindly bouncing from one rendition of your ineffective solution to another and simply prolonging the problem.

If you have already leapt to a solution, however, you can use it to back yourself into a good definition. Let's return to Ted and watch how he does this:

LUCY: "Ted, you said that Harry should be sent back to corporate or fired. If he were, what problem would you no longer have to face?"

TED: "His rotten attitude. I just hate listening to his constant chorus of 'You have to do this for me' and 'I have to have all the data before I can send you what you asked for.' When I push him about what specific data he needs, or tell him to trust me when I ask for, say, a copy of a program, he just repeats, 'I need all the data first; I just need the data.' Then he'll add: 'I have to know what's going on; you have to talk with me before you implement anything.' Who does he think he is, the CEO? God?"

LUCY: "Hmmm. Is your main problem with Harry that he's constantly asking for more information rather than just taking your word that you need something?"

TED: "Not just asking for information, but not telling me exactly what information he needs and why he needs it. He demands to know everything—as if he were the sole decision maker in this company. He's like an old-style controller—counting every penny, trying to become the funnel through which all knowledge flows. I hate his trying to control everything. His style will limit the future of this company."

LUCY: "So it's not just asking for a lot of information, but not telling you specifically what he needs and why. And he does so in a demanding manner. Is that your main concern?"

TED: "Yes."

Before, Ted was only thinking about what should happen to Harry, and was not focused on the particular behavior he wanted

Harry to change. Now he has a better handle on what Harry specifically does and says that bugs him, which is a much more manageable problem than his original list of laments. With this information he can address the actual problem and find a solution he has the power to implement.

The following exercise will help you identify a premature solution.

AVOIDING THE DEAD END

1. Notice what you're saying or thinking about your problem. Write down your comments or thoughts that start with phrases like: "I should . . . ," "She should . . . ," "The best way to take care of this is . . . ," "The only thing to do is . . . ," "I have to . . . ," "I need to . . . ," "I must . . . ," "My only choice is . . . ." These describe solutions, not problems. For example, Ted's list would include "Harry should be fired."
2. Ask yourself about each sentence you wrote down: What problem is that solution supposed to handle? If that solution worked, what problem would it fix? Your answer should clarify your problem. For Ted, Harry's being fired was supposed to solve the problem of having to cope with Harry's demands for information.
3. Now focus on your answer to step two, which will be a better statement of your problem, and flesh out that definition by answering the four questions: 1) who; 2) does what; 3) to whom; and 4) how is it a problem?

The Straight (But Not So Narrow) Path

With a little practice, getting people to change isn't all that complicated. But people rarely change their annoying behavior spontaneously. After all, their behavior bothers you, not them, and so you have to instigate the change. If you've unsuccessfully prodded them to change, you can easily lose track of the dance steps that make up the actual problem. This makes you vulnerable to repeating your ineffective solution, which, of course, then feeds your problem. Taking the time to clearly describe your frustrating situation will show you the way out of your difficulties.

The path to a clear definition of your problem is crosshatched with detours—explanations, speculations, labels, and instant solutions. You can successfully avoid these detours by sticking to the facts and describing your problem this way:

Who is doing
> **what** that presents a problem,
>> **to whom,** and
>>> **how** is this behavior a problem?

This tells you precisely what you are trying to change, which will make it much easier to succeed. With this information, you have completed step one: What is the primary problem?

In the next chapter, we move to the second question in the process: What have you been doing about your problem so far? You'll discover what specific solution you keep repeating that has become your part in the dance (the more you . . . , the more they do the same annoying things). You'll learn how to identify it and what to do instead.

FIVE

Shall We *Not* Dance: Taking the Lead

The instructors started the western dance lessons by announcing, "We don't care how you live your private lives, but on the dance floor, the man leads." Then they floated about the floor, showing us the Texas two-step. My husband and I tried to imitate them but ended up with what could only be described as the Texas toe-stomp. It was pitiful. I strongly suspected that if my husband would just lead with a bit more courage, we wouldn't be having this trouble. Then an instructor stopped us and wanted to talk to me: "There's no way your husband can lead because every time he tries, your arms go as limp as cooked noodles. Keep them locked and firm."

I hate it when that happens! It was much more fun when it was all my husband's fault. On the other hand, dancing a snappy Texas two-step was much more fun than being right.

You Mean It's Not the Other Guy?

It takes some fortitude to stop focusing on the other guy who is really bugging you and start reviewing your own actions instead. Let's say that your micromanaging supervisor drives you crazy with increasing demands for reports and reviews. To get her to change, you must stop focusing on how she should quit asking for so much information. Instead you must look at what *you* keep doing that seems to elicit these continued demands from her. You need to make a deliberate effort to change the focus of your attention from what your infuriating supervisor does over and over to what you yourself do over and over.

When you succeed in shifting your focus, you will discover the magic of this process:

> To get someone to change his or her frustrating behavior, just change what *you* are doing.

To figure out what to do differently, you first need to identify the common thread in all your seemingly diverse but ineffective efforts. You start by answering this question:

What, in your best efforts, have you tried to get someone to change?

Judy from chapter two, who was dissatisfied with her warehouseman Rob because he would never listen to his employees, made this list:

- Talked with Rob repeatedly about listening to his staff's ideas,
- Made "Listen more effectively" a performance goal in his performance appraisal,
- Observed his staff meetings and made suggestions for listening better,
- Sent him to a training program on listening skills.

Judy's numerous efforts to fix her problem with Rob appeared diverse to her. However, once she studied what all her efforts had in common, she discovered a common thread. Judy's exertions all boiled down to repeating this basic statement: "You can and should listen to your employees."

She tried to get her theme across in several ways, some more direct than others. Judy would say to Rob:

- "You should listen better!"
- "You treat your employees like pieces of furniture."
- "You never listen."
- "Why don't you pay attention to your employees?"

Judy also tried to get her theme across in indirect ways: sighing loudly in disgust, blowing up in anger, leaving books about listening skills on Rob's desk, and signing him up for listening skills training.

Even though Judy had tried every way she could think of to get her message across, Rob didn't change. But she kept trying, thus taking the two steps that prolong rather than extinguish unwanted behavior: 1) She chose a solution that didn't work; and 2) when the problem wasn't resolved, she continued doing more of the same. Her repeated efforts created this waltz:

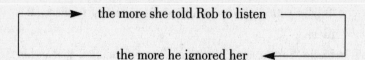

the more she told Rob to listen

the more he ignored her

To change the dance, just change your own dance steps. When Judy avoided conveying this message—in any form—she stopped the dance. She tried a very different tune and told Rob: "While I've been preaching at you to listen to your workers, it's occurred to me that it's mainly your talented workers who are leaving your unit. While the turnover makes it harder for you since you're working shorthanded all the time, I think your style encourages the good workers to stretch their wings and try new jobs in the organization. The other units benefit, so maybe you shouldn't listen after all."

This very different approach broke the more-of-the-same cycle and got through to Rob, who began to pay more attention to his staff's comments. Morale improved and the turnover stopped.

Figuring Out the Dance

To get the hang of this, let's look in on Katherine, the regional sales manager from chapter three, who can't get guidance from her boss on important projects. In the following conversation, we sketch out her part in the dance and, once that is done, a new strategy becomes apparent.

CONVERSATION	ANALYSIS
LUCY: "You said that the trouble you're having with this current assignment is typical of your problem with your boss, mainly that you can't get his guidance on assignments. Let's look at what you have tried so far in order to get his help. What have you said or done? What hasn't worked or hasn't worked well enough—that is, has only worked temporarily?	*We need to see how Katherine had attempted to change him so we can identify the theme she must now avoid. What has she been doing over and over that is now inadvertently reinforcing her boss's behavior?*
KATHERINE: "Well, nothing has worked. I set up appointments through his assistant, but my boss usually cancels them at the last minute. I catch him in the hallway and ask to see him. He says to set up an appointment, and then rushes off. Eventually we always find a time to meet, but when we do, he doesn't give me the information I need, and brushes me off."	*She describes a series of things she's tried and what his reactions were. She sets up appointments, he cancels. She catches him in the hallway, he rushes off. They meet, he doesn't give her information, "brushes her off." She is beginning to describe the dance between them.*

LUCY: "What do you mean by 'brushes you off'?"

If you don't describe specific behaviors, you will have trouble seeing what's actually going on. Then it will be hard to figure out what to do differently. She needs to describe what he does that she vaguely labels "brushes her off."

KATHERINE: "Well, he'll launch into some parable that I am supposed to glean 'truth' from. Or he'll go off on some rambling philosophical lecture, as if he were a college professor. I try to pin him down, but he'll say something like 'I'm sure you know what I'm getting at.' Then he'll start shuffling papers and make it clear the meeting is over."

"Brushes her off" means not directly answering her questions and then signaling the end of the meeting. So another move in their dance is Katherine's asking her boss a question that he doesn't answer directly.

LUCY: "What do you say or do to try to 'pin him down' or to get the answers from him that you need?"

Again I'm requesting a specific description of her own actions, her efforts to change him. What does she actually say or do that might trigger his vague responses?

At this stage the question you must keep in the forefront is: What are you doing that may inadvertently cue the annoying behavior?

KATHERINE: "Well, frankly, by the time he's finished with his lecture, I'm so confused by his rambling and so tired of his condescension that I just want to get out of there. But I'll say something like 'Is there anything I should know about this assignment?' Or 'Is there anything else you can tell me?' Or I'll ask him how far he wants me to go with the assignment, if I am headed in the right direction—things like that. He'll respond with some vague statement like 'You should use your own judgment on that.' Then I give up and leave. I'm afraid he'll think I'm incompetent if I ask too many questions."

So Katherine continues to ask general questions and he continues to respond vaguely. She keeps asking questions, though, even when he's signaled that he's through with the conversation. At this stage, a pattern is beginning to take shape, but we're not quite there yet. You'll probably find the same situation when working on your own dance. You have to delve for details before you will discover the steps of the dance.

LUCY: "You said he responds to your questions with a vague lecture or parable. Give me an example of the questions you ask that may lead him to lecture or give a parable. What do you say to him? Think of a recent episode, if you can."

An example demonstrates what's actually said or done and helps you avoid useless generalities, judgments, and vague labels. A recent example keeps you from solving an old problem. (Problems with people evolve—you want to fix the rendition you currently face.)

KATHERINE: "Well, when we met last week, I needed to know if I was on track with my survey. I asked him what he thought about the idea of surveying all the divisions for my report. He looked kind of surprised, then sat back and rambled on and on about the value and the pitfalls of surveys."

She asks about "the idea" of surveying, which is another general question. This triggers another vague response.

LUCY: "Let me see if I've got the picture. You set up appointments, he cancels. You catch him in the hall, he rushes off. You ask a question, he gives a vague response or a lecture. You try to pin him down, he ends the meeting."

Can you ferret out what Katherine has been doing over and over? What implied statement is Katherine making repeatedly about what her boss should do?

KATHERINE: "Yes, that's about it."

LUCY: "It sounds to me like your message to him has been, in effect, 'I'm waiting for you to give me the direction you should give me.' But he doesn't give direction, so you try again, and again. I think the dance is this: You pursue him in various ways to get his guidance, but he evades. You pursue some more, he evades some more.

So the theme of Katherine's ineffective efforts is "You should give me direction." She continually pursues her boss to try and get it. Pursue/evade, pursue/evade, grab your partner and do-si-do.

KATHERINE: "Well, yes, I guess so. I mean, I think it's his job to give clear direction. It certainly would help."

This is part of Katherine's "story" that keeps her stuck: It's his job to give direction. It's logical, probably even accurate. But it doesn't help her figure out how to get that guidance. It only lets her feel somewhat righteous.

LUCY: "OK, but clearly pursuing him or bugging him doesn't work—not with him. It's as if he plays hard to get."

While logical, her solution isn't working, and sets up the dance:

    the more she pursues

      the more he evades

KATHERINE: "That's exactly what it feels like! It's infuriating."

LUCY: "All right. So you'll have to do something very different from pursuing him, different from saying, in effect, 'You must give me direction.' It's not that there is anything wrong with what you were doing—it's just that it doesn't work with him, and makes him shy away. What could you do that would be quite different from pushing for his direction, different from implying he should give you guidance?"

In other words, more pursuit simply won't work! Not with this manager. So she must avoid that solution if she wants him to change. She must change the dance by doing something significantly different.

KATHERINE: "I could ignore him. Or tell him to drop dead. Well, no, I couldn't do that, but I could just give up on him and go about my business as best I can. Makes me nervous, though, to proceed without help."

Katherine comes up with a solution that is more like withdrawing from the problem than trying to fix it. You may find yourself, at this stage, strongly tempted to do the same thing. Resist. It won't work. For example, her suggestion would not actively deal with the problem and so her frustration would grow as she withdrew and waited silently for guidance. Soon her frustration and nervousness would draw her back into the dance— back to her old pursuit. She needs to take an active step that will break up the old dance routine and increase the odds of getting the needed guidance.

LUCY: "I'm not suggesting you go off half-cocked without some guidance. We just need to figure out a way to get you the help you need, a way genuinely different from your previous attempts. If you just ignore him, since he's so busy he may not notice for a while. But the opposite of pursuing is not ignoring but is actively not pursuing. For instance, what if you were to tell him—in a brief exchange in the hallway or a quick stop at his office—that you realize you've been a pest, but for him not to worry, that you've got everything figured out on your own. Then walk away. What do you think his reaction would be?"

KATHERINE: "Relief. But on the other hand, that might make him very nervous. He wouldn't know what I was going to do. Oh, interesting. In other words, *I'm* the one who plays hard to get."

I suggest a new dance, one that might get her boss to wonder what she's doing. Let his curiosity draw him to her instead of her pushing and pursuing—which he resists. At the very least, the new tactic tells her boss he has no need to avoid her anymore.

To break up the dance, figure out the opposite of your previous routine. Your new efforts must be very different from the old theme. The opposite is a good place to begin your planning.

LUCY: "In a way, yes. You'd stop
what doesn't work—pursuit—
and instead tell him you're
backing off and going on about
your business, giving him a
chance to see what he needs
to do."

KATHERINE: "I like it. It's
certainly worth a try."

Katherine caught her boss in the hallway and tried out her new strategy. Later, when she passed him in the hall, she just said hello and kept walking—resisting her urge to again question him. To her surprise her boss dropped by within a couple of days to see what she was doing on the project. She explained her plans, but didn't ask him questions. He responded by offering a number of helpful suggestions and she got the guidance she needed.

How did it work? Katherine altered the balance of power with her small but important change in the dance. Her boss could no longer do-si-do when she whirled off into the macarena.

What's Your Part in the Dance?

To identify your theme, or your part in the dance, review your ineffective efforts. Most of them will fit in one pattern. They will be different ways of delivering the same statement about what someone should or should not do (or feel). Your part in the dance will consist of all the different ways you try to pound that one message into the other person's head.

Don't be discouraged if initially you have trouble identifying the theme. Detecting the basic statement you've been repeating is like solving a puzzle. What you'll need are clear descriptions of what you've said and done so you can *see* what you've been doing. Then you can answer the question:

> What is the basic statement you are making about what this person should or should not do, or should or should not feel?

The following exercise will help you identify your theme.

IDENTIFYING YOUR THEME

Refer to the problem you've defined in the previous exercises.

1. List all the ways that you've tried to get someone to change his or her behavior.
2. Make sure that you've listed behaviors—what you've said or done—rather than labels ("I was conciliatory") or reasons or speculations. Use the troubleshooting steps in chapter four to double-check yourself. (You'll find them summarized on page 68.)
3. Read the list over several times and ask yourself: What am I trying to get through to this person? What is the basic statement I am making about what this person should or should not do, or should or should not feel?

    If you're working to change a habit or fear of your own, ask yourself: What is it I am telling myself that I should or should not do, or should or should not feel?

Once you recognize your theme, you'll know what to avoid when you pick a new strategy. The next chapter will describe five basic themes that people tend to use over and over. In effect, most of us know only five dances. You're about to learn what they are and several ways to change the steps.

The Usual Suspects: Common-sense Solutions That Don't Work

You've lined up your target: the specific behavior you intend to get changed. You're tired of the More-of-the-Same Dance and ready to give it up. But what to give up? Perhaps you're not quite sure what, exactly, you're doing over and over. None of your solutions seem related. Not to worry.

Sorting out what strategy to dump is the trickiest part of this model, but luckily there are only five fundamental strategies that cause most of our grief. As Dr. Dick Fisch, a psychiatrist for more than forty years, put it: "People really aren't all that creative when it comes to problems. There just aren't that many ways people get themselves into trouble."

So if you can't get your spouse to stop working late, your assistant to show up on time, or your son to clean up his room, chances are that you're repeating one of these ineffective solutions: 1) repeatedly urging them to change; 2) trying to talk them into liking your request; 3) demanding acknowledgment that you're right; 4) using the indirect approach; or 5) trying to conquer your fear with endless preparation. Even if your strategy doesn't fit into one of these categories, knowing "the usual suspects" will help you figure yours out. And as likely as not, your nonproductive strategy is one of the regular culprits in disguise. Keep in mind, though, that any repeated tactic that doesn't get you the desired change should be regarded as perpetuating the unwanted behavior. Chapters six through ten will look at these ineffective solutions one at a time.

SIX

The Ear That Doesn't Hear:
Repeatedly Urging Change

With this strategy, your efforts revolve around repeatedly urging someone to change. You ask, encourage, suggest, plead, demand, beseech, beg, threaten, whine, and cajole, all to no avail.

- "Clean up your room. It's a disaster area!"
- "You've got to be at work on time. We've talked about this a hundred times before."
- "Honey, you've got to stop working such long hours. You're going to kill yourself."

Sometimes such statements work. Your son considers your request, finds it reasonable, and cleans up his room. In your dreams. But if you and your son are normal, you carp and he whines, you yell and he pouts, and, well, you know the routine.

Even when you dust off your notes from Communications Skills 101 and state your case perfectly, your urging doesn't work. Your spouse still works fourteen-hour days. Your employee still shows up late with a new excuse each week. And your son still wades merrily through the piles on his bedroom floor. This predicament is not that unusual; many people would rather put up with someone's grousing than change their own habits.

When urging doesn't work, it is tempting, if only in utter frustration, to repeat your pleas. After all, your requests are reasonable and you have the right to make them. Therefore you continue to implore your wife to work less, telling her how good it would be for her career or her health (or your marriage) if she changed. But she doesn't. You've become Poor Johnny One Note and it isn't working. All your efforts boil down to one basic theme—repeatedly urging her to change in spite of the fact that your urging doesn't work. It's even possible that your wife, dreading the inevitable argument, now dawdles even longer at work. Your part in the dance now guarantees that she won't listen to you:

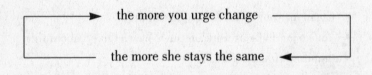

the more you urge change

the more she stays the same

But Now What?

What to do instead? First of all, stop urging. It was worth a try, but you've tested this approach thoroughly and it doesn't work. And it didn't fail because you stated your case poorly. You know you tried a dozen ways to say your piece. At this point, no matter how well you polish your next speech, it would still be more urging. You now have to do something completely different.

Your new approach must accomplish two things. First, it must change the rhythm of the dance so the dance can no longer continue as before. Second, your new approach must be different enough from the old routine to trigger the change you want.

The following are several ways to break out of this "urging" dance and get the change you want. Some of these entail simple and logical changes in tactics. Others are counterintuitive and will probably give you pause. They are so, well, different. But if your partner keeps dancing the waltz, you have to strike out with some different steps, the Electric Slide, perhaps? Yes, it doesn't work with the waltz. That's the point.

All of the following solutions have been tried by my clients and they work. Glean what you can from them as you go along and we'll tackle how to tailor them for your own use in a later chapter.

1. TELL SOMEONE *NOT* TO CHANGE

Kevin and Carol, trainers for the Environmental Protection Agency in Washington, D.C., needed to deliver ten sessions of technical training. After the third session Kevin was completely frustrated with Carol, who trained well but often took forty-five minutes to deliver a twenty-minute lecture. To get them back on schedule, Kevin would cut his own lectures short. Often they stayed late revising the next day's schedule to fit in leftover training. Carol, apologizing, always promised to pay closer attention to the clock the next time, but she never did. Frustrated, Kevin asked for my help. He explained the problem, which we diagrammed this way:

- ***Who:*** Carol
- *is doing **what:*** repeatedly lecturing too long and throwing the schedule off

- **_to whom_** _it's a problem:_ Kevin (not to the participants or to Carol)
- **_how_** _her behavior is a problem:_ He rushes his own lectures and no longer enjoys training, stays late to work on the schedule, and resents the time taken from his family.

To sketch out the dance, I asked Kevin, "In trying to get Carol to keep to the schedule, what have you tried so far that _hasn't_ worked?"

He replied, "I've talked with her and explained the impact on both the program and on me when she lectures for too long. I've sat in the back of the room and pointed to the clock when she's running over. I've reminded her just before she starts a lecture that she promised to keep to the schedule. I've scowled at her when she blows it. I've refused to cut my lectures short in the afternoon to accommodate her overrun from the morning. But then we work late redesigning the next day's schedule. She doesn't mind working late, but I do. Oh, she always apologizes, but then she turns around and does the same thing the next day!"

Kevin's Theme

Kevin had described his varied efforts clearly, and with a little reflection, we figured out the common thread that ran through them all. In various ways, Kevin has repeatedly told Carol, "You can and should stick to the schedule." This obviously didn't work, in spite of his perseverance. So now we could see his part in their dance:

> the more Kevin urges her to stick to the schedule

> the more she ignores the schedule

Since ineffectual urging like Kevin's is such a common error, it may be the very one that you're repeating. Think about the employee you've been pestering about his late project, or the colleague you've been warning about his sloppy work, or the cubicle mate you've been nagging about her endless phone calls. What basic statement have you been making over and over? Since it hasn't worked, that statement—no matter how skillfully you deliver it—is now part of the problem. Just like with Kevin, knowing what *not* to do is more than half the battle.

No Need to Change

Now that Kevin knew what to avoid, we could begin devising a plan. Since looking at consequences is one way to come up with some interesting ideas, I asked Kevin, "What happens when she ignores your requests? What are the consequences for her of lecturing overtime?"

He replied, "For her? Not much. She has to deal with my grumbling and scowling, but that doesn't seem to be any big deal for her. She doesn't mind working late. I'm the one who pays the price: Either I cut short my lectures and don't enjoy the training or I work late night after night redesigning, which I really resent."

So Kevin is actually covering for her. With no consequences for her, there's not much reason to change. Enduring Kevin's grumbling is apparently a small price to pay.

It's not unusual for people to keep urging change and not think about consequences. Even parents and managers often don't use the obvious consequences available to them—perhaps for fear that the employee will quit or that the child will make life more miserable. But I also think there's a loss of perspective at play. For instance, someone annoys you and you ask him to change. He doesn't. You figure he didn't understand you or didn't understand the importance of your request, so you ask again. Nothing happens. You try again. As you keep investing time and energy, your frustration grows. When you finally think about consequences, they're generally in the category of "I could just strangle him!" But since that's not an option, you go back to talking. You're back in the same old dance and don't see other possibilities.

But there are many consequences far short of murder, and small ones can be just as powerful as major ones. Let's see what Kevin did.

Kevin knew he had to avoid telling Carol to stick to the schedule and had to stop rescuing her when she blew it. He grumbled, "I could just give up on getting her to change and let her lecture for as long as she wants. I mean, that's what's happening anyway. Then I could do my own lectures as originally planned, in a relaxed way instead of trying to make up time. When she runs over, I could let her stay late to do the redesign without me."

Kevin is getting close: Quit telling her to keep to the schedule and don't make up her lost time. But I was worried about his tone of voice. If he said something sarcastic, like "Lecture all day if you want!" he would still be sending the same old ineffective theme.

The New Plan

As a way of fleshing out Kevin's idea, I asked him: "What if you let go of your wish for her to change and just got on with enjoying your own training? What do you think would happen?" He said, "Well, truth be told, I'm a little envious of her relaxed style. She's great with the participants and looks like she's having such a good time. I think that's why I'm so resentful of having to rush my own lectures to play catch-up."

This is useful new information. Sometimes surprising feelings or thoughts pop up as you muddle around searching for something different to try. And do expect to muddle. You're weaning yourself from a solution that seems so right—except, of course, that it doesn't work. It takes a little fussing with ideas before most of us can see beyond the old tried-but-untrue.

Kevin's answer gave me an idea for a strategy different from his old one—the opposite, as a matter of fact (a tactic we'll explore further in chapter seven). I suggested a solution designed to jolt Carol out of her usual comfort zone: "You know, Kevin, if you really want out of this mess, you should tell Carol that you want to be as relaxed as she is with the classes. Tell her that from now on you intend to learn to train as well as she does. If you said that, you would avoid the old routine of 'You should stick to the schedule' and instead you would, in effect, be saying to her, 'Take as much time as you want.' "

Kevin said, "I'll try it. At the very least, my stomach won't be in such a knot at the end of the day."

Kevin did try it, telling Carol he envied her training style and intended to see if he could learn to be as relaxed. He apologized for being so uptight about the schedule (a dramatically different message from his previous one) and announced that he was turning over a new leaf. He then relaxed and gave his own lectures more or less within the time allotted, not rushing to get the schedule back on track. He quit worrying about the clock and began to enjoy himself. When Carol lectured overtime, Kevin went home on time, telling her to fix the next day's schedule any way she wanted.

To his relief, Carol began to worry about the schedule, and soon was sticking much closer to the time lines. His new approach got Carol to change. Their teamwork and the training flowed much more smoothly.

It Worked, But How?

How did this work? It's as if you're paddling a canoe across a lake, and the canoe is moving at a nice pace. You then notice that your companion has put down her oar and is gazing at the scenery. You keep paddling and ask her to help out. She doesn't. Resentful, you continue to paddle, all the while urging her to pick up her oar. But why should she? You're getting the job done. If you stop urging her to help and instead begin trailing your own oar in the water, what happens to the canoe? If she wants to get to shore (which she will eventually), she'll need to pick up her oar and paddle. If urging doesn't work, try something else. Kevin stopped paddling and, in effect, said to Carol, "I think you've got the right idea. You know, I hadn't even noticed the scenery. What a beautiful day!"

When you focus on changing your own actions, you can usually figure out how to get the other person to change hers. And, as long as you avoid more urging, there are a number of solutions that will work. Kevin showed you one—telling Carol to stay the same while letting the natural consequences of her behavior land on her. Kelly used another: creating consequences.

2. CREATE CONSEQUENCES

Kelly, senior vice president of a large health care organization, had a problem with Jake, her brilliant and talented vice president of accounting. Jake had the intimidating habit of chewing out his managers in the hallway and of haranguing and insulting employees at meetings. Kelly tried to get Jake to change, but he continued to badger people and yell at them.

Kelly didn't want to lose this talented, albeit flawed, man and wasn't willing to fire him. But Jake's managers were demoralized and Kelly found out that several of them were thinking about quitting.

Kelly's problem:

- **Who:** Jake
- *is doing what:* yelling at and insulting his managers
- *to whom:* his managers and other employees at meetings
- *how this is a problem:* The managers are angry and demoralized and are threatening to quit.

Her unsuccessful efforts to get Jake to change:

- Talked with Jake numerous times about his unacceptable behavior, both casually and in meetings specifically for that purpose;
- Made it a goal in Jake's yearly performance appraisal to improve his treatment of people;
- Even lost her temper and yelled at him about his treatment of people.

Her part in the dance became clear: With talks, performance appraisals, and yelling, Kelly kept repeating her theme that Jake "should treat people better."

It's not that Kelly chose the wrong things to do. Sometimes these steps are effective. But when urging doesn't work, more urging won't work either. Then it's time to stop polishing your next speech and do something significantly different—like creating consequences. If there are no natural consequences, you can create them.

You Want Me to Do What?

At first Kelly didn't feel she could impose consequences. "Consequences? I can't fire him. He's too talented to lose. The board would never approve." Like Kelly, many of us think mainly of severe consequences, like firing. But there are a number of possibilities far short of firing. Consequences should simply make someone pay a price for not changing his behavior.

The very next week Kelly assigned to another manager a treasured annual project that usually went to Jake. When Jake stormed into her office to protest, Kelly calmly explained, "Having to control your temper would be a big burden for you on this project, so I've assigned it to someone else." And then she ended the conversation.

Kelly didn't deliver her usual lecture about treating people better (although she was sorely tempted to). Nor did she again tell Jake that he should change. In fact, her words implied that, while he was capable of change, she didn't expect him to (". . . would be a big burden for you"), and so she would simply work around that. She said all this with a calm tone, letting the consequences speak for themselves. If she'd used an exasperated tone of voice, her tone would have implied the same old ineffective theme that he should change. Instead, she stopped her part in the dance completely and let her actions say to him, "You don't want to paddle the canoe? That's OK. I'll just deposit you on the shore where you won't need to and I'll put someone else in the boat." This approach got Jake's attention in a hurry and his treatment of people improved markedly.

Creating consequences is a second solution very different from continually exhorting someone to change. Keep in mind that the use of consequences frees you to depart from your ineffective reminding, exhorting, struggling—the tack that has kept you in the dance. Thus, consequences need not be severe. You'll see examples of other effective consequences later in the book.

3. ENCOURAGE SOMEONE TO DO IT MORE

But what if you're not in a position to set up consequences, say, with a difficult colleague? Here's another option that, at first blush, may seem outlandish, but can be very effective. This strategy is based on the fact that, in these ongoing battles to get others to change, you usually become quite predictable. Your manager or colleague or best friend knows what you will say and so can ignore your words as successfully as you ignored your parents' carping as a child. So you need to do something unexpected—something that will throw them off their game, so to speak. For example, what do you think would happen if, instead of urging someone to change his troublesome behavior, you encouraged him to do it even more? Sound crazy?

My father used this technique when faced with a child's temper tantrum. For example, he would watch everyone else try to placate or soothe little Timmy, the neighbor's child. In response, Timmy would only holler louder. The more others urged the child to quiet down, basically telling him "You should not feel upset," the louder Timmy squalled. Then my father would step in. He'd go up to him and say, "Oh, c'mon. Is that the best you can do? That's not much of a yell. Surely you can yell louder than that! Now give it your best shot. C'mon, let's really hear it—louder! Louder!" And little Timmy would glower at him, hiccup, and stop.

Jeanette, regional sales manager for a Midwest chemical

company, used this method to handle a very prickly peer, Gwen, who belittled everyone during staff meetings. Gwen would sarcastically interrupt her peers' reports with comments like "Do we really have to listen to any more of this? Let's move on." Jeanette had told Gwen often how disruptive this was, as had Gwen's boss. But Gwen continued, in meeting after meeting, to tear apart everyone's reports.

Jeanette's repeated theme was urging Gwen to change her disruptive behavior (and urging her boss to urge Gwen to change). That didn't work. So Jeanette stopped her part in the dance. She quit urging and instead tried something quite different. She pointed out to Gwen that their boss seemed to view Jeanette's work much more sympathetically when Gwen attacked it and so she would appreciate Gwen's continuing her criticism. At the very next meeting, when Gwen launched into her usual tirade about Jeanette's work, Jeanette sat quietly. Then, after the meeting, Jeanette thanked her for the help and walked away, leaving Gwen standing in the hall looking puzzled.

Never Change a Winning Game

In the following meeting, Gwen tempered her behavior somewhat. So Jeanette—to reinforce her success—mentioned in passing after the meeting that she was disappointed in Gwen. If Gwen stopped attacking her work, Jeanette would have to come to these meetings better prepared and she'd prefer that Gwen save her the extra work. Gwen backed off more each week and became more reasonable in meetings, most of the time anyway. When Gwen forgot herself and ranted and raved again, Jeanette would quietly smile and then thank Gwen after the meeting, short-circuiting Gwen's return to her old habits. In effect,

Jeanette not only stopped asking Gwen to paddle the canoe, she pointed out how good it made Jeanette look to their boss when Gwen didn't paddle and let her do it all. That broke up the dance.

It may seem strange that encouraging people to continue their irritating behavior would get them to stop it. But if you have been repeatedly urging them to change and no change occurs, then you must quit pushing the old theme and do something very different, not just another variation on urging change. If you keep urging at this point, you will prolong the problem:

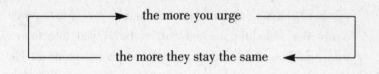

the more you urge

the more they stay the same

Again, your new approach must accomplish two things. First, it must change the rhythm of the dance so it can no longer continue as before. Second, your new approach must be different enough from the old routine to trigger the change you want.

As you'll see in chapter nine, there are times when directly asking someone to change is appropriate and effective. But if you've tried this approach repeatedly and it hasn't worked, then this is not one of those times. To get the change you're seeking, you'll need to stop urging and instead try something else, something very different.

In Summary

You've seen three ways to break up the Urging Dance: 1) tell someone not to change; 2) create consequences or let the natural consequences occur; and 3) urge someone to do the annoying actions even more. When you let go of your futile efforts, you can invent others that are successful. Your new solution doesn't need to be elaborate, just different.

Here's an exercise to help you figure out what to do instead of endlessly urging someone to change.

WHEN URGING DOESN'T WORK

1. Consider consequences. Ask yourself:

    Do you protect someone from the consequences of his or her behavior? Kevin always rushed his training to make sure the schedule worked out, or he stayed late to re-design. Therefore, Carol suffered no consequences. He quit doing that and let the natural consequences of her behavior land on her instead of him.

    Is there any compelling reason for the person to change? If not, what compelling consequences can you create? Kelly took a prized project away from Jake since "controlling his temper would be a burden for him."

2. Look for a hidden feeling beneath your expressed feeling. For Kevin, his resentment of his co-trainer Carol obscured his envy of her relaxed training style. Discovering the envy led to the notion of telling her that he wanted to learn from her and that she should "take all the time she wanted"—the opposite of saying, "You must stick to the schedule."

3. Think about urging the person to continue the annoying behavior. For instance, Jeanette pointed out to Gwen that her boss gave Jeanette's work a more favorable review when Gwen blasted it. (For another twist on this method,

remember how Tom Sawyer got the other boys to white-
wash the fence for him and even pay him for the "privi-
lege.") To put a new light on your situation, ask yourself:
What are the advantages to you of this current problem?

Keep in mind that the issue isn't whether your solution should
work, or even whether it has worked before in other circum-
stances. If you can't get someone to change, then the way you're
going about it has become an integral part of your dance together and perpetuates the problem. To get the change you want,
change your part in the dance.

Let's look at another dance you may occasionally find yourself stuck in.

SEVEN

You Should-Oughta-Wanna Like This: Trying to Talk Someone into Liking Your Request

With the should-oughta-wanna approach, you are again asking people to change. As with the "urging" solution, you are talking too much, only this time you're trying to talk people into agreeing that your request is fair and reasonable and therefore they should-oughta-wanna do it. You act as if you aren't really demanding compliance—you want them to *want* to change. (You may remember your mother using this approach when she told you that you didn't really want ice cream before dinner.)

Parents can inadvertently get caught in this dance when telling a child no. Mark and Sarah didn't want their daughter to go to the movies on a school night. But rather than simply saying no, they began the steps they often danced whenever their daughter didn't like their decision. They worked to convince her that she should like their decision, or at least agree with it. ("You don't want to go to the movies. You'll get home too late, you'll be too tired for school tomorrow. You said you wanted to finish your history report, and besides, I'm too tired to drive you to the theater . . .") The daughter, predictably, did not say "OK, I see the logic of your decision and I graciously agree." Instead, she tirelessly debated each reason they presented. ("I'm almost through with that report and I can finish it in study hall tomorrow. I won't be too tired. The movie's over at nine-thirty and you've let me stay up that late before. I'll get Mary's mother to drive us. . . .")

Sarah and Mark wanted her to comply with their decision. But they also wanted her to *want* to comply, and that's where they got hooked into the dance:

> the more they tried to get her to like their decision

> the more she resisted and argued

Continuing to try and reason with the daughter, in an effort to get her agreement, will do no good at this point. It will only prolong the debate. She may comply and not go to the movies, but there's not much chance of her agreeing that no is the right answer. To break up this dance, Mark and Sarah would need to forget logical arguments and instead simply say no. They could also break up the dance by coming up with a totally illogical reason for saying no, such as, "No, you can't go because the moon will be full that night" or "because we are terrible parents." You can bet the daughter won't disagree with that one. When you stop feeding it with reasons, the frustrating debate ends.

This routine is played out similarly in business. Let's say that Corporate issues a new policy that you know your employees will detest. You also know that you have no choice about implementing this policy. You arm yourself against your employees' protests with reasons for why they should like this policy, how pleased they should be that the company is thinking ahead, how good it will be for the department in the long run, yada yada yada. As you'd predicted, they spit back all the reasons as to why this policy is a real loser, that Corporate has no grip on reality, that you can't possibly expect them to comply. You will continue the dance if you keep trying to talk them into liking the policy:

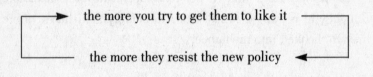

They don't need to like it or even agree with it. They need to comply. The same routine may fuel the endless discussions with your tardy employee who has a thousand reasons for why he shouldn't have to be at his desk at the prescribed time. He doesn't need to like coming to work on time; he just needs to do it.

If you find yourself constantly working to convince people that they should agree with or like a change, and yet nothing changes, stop. More of the same will only result in more resistance liberally seasoned with grumbling. To get the change implemented, you have to do something else.

First, decide if the change—whether it's compliance with a new policy or a request for a change in someone's behavior—is open to negotiation or not. If yes, then discussion and argument are appropriate. But if the change is nonnegotiable and action must be taken, then state simply and clearly what needs to be done. That doesn't mean that you completely ignore people's feelings about the matter. Things usually go more smoothly if you concede that the task is unpleasant or a pain, but that nevertheless it must be done. Then move on quickly to discussing how to implement the change.

A variation on this theme is pretending that employees can influence a decision when, in fact, the decision has already been made. Tomás, a vice president at a pharmaceutical company in North Carolina, knew the specific decision he wanted to make. But to get his project leaders to like and support the decision, he thought they should "feel" involved. He held a meeting ostensibly to get their views, but then objected to every idea they presented (except the one he wanted). The meeting lasted just as long as it took Tomás to maneuver them around to his decision. He got the decision he wanted, although he later found that the commitment to implement that decision was sorely lacking. Tomás also found very little enthusiasm for discussing the next decision he claimed was theirs to make.

Sometimes, you're on the receiving end of this routine. Your colleague continually overwhelms you with reasons for why you should-oughta-wanna do something. You can stop the dance by simply interrupting your colleague and saying, "Just tell me what you want me to do."

EIGHT

One-Upsmanship: Demanding Acknowledgment That You're Right

We all live or work in relationships that require mutual cooperation. It is when we find ourselves at odds with someone whose cooperation we need that the third ineffective solution comes into play. The trouble usually starts with an ordinary disagreement. While healthy arguments can produce new ideas and better decisions, when one party tries to win the argument by acting superior, things can quickly turn ugly. It's classic one-upsmanship: using displays of superiority to try and gain the advantage.

When someone takes the one-up position ("You call that a workable proposal? That's the stupidest idea I've ever heard!"), the other person feels "put down," that the legitimacy of his position has been denied or that he has been treated with disrespect. He is unlikely to respond, "Why, thank you! I thought my idea was pretty stupid, too." Rather, he will probably try to even up the relationship, demanding in various ways to be treated as if he is one-up. For instance, he may badger the other person to admit the legitimacy of his position, in effect saying, "You should admit that I'm right and you're wrong." Or "You should defer to my views on the matter." This, of course, rarely works, as the person holding the one-up position tends to hang on to it. The conflict escalates as one person continues to act superior or one-up while the other continues to demand acknowledgment of his position. It becomes an adult-style king of the hill.

It is not uncommon to feel put down or unappreciated in the course of working (or living) with someone, so even minor differences of opinion can elicit this one-upsmanship solution and lead to a protracted conflict. This is what happened to Charles and Peter, division vice presidents and peers in a mid-size manufacturing company in Colorado, whose conflict began as many do—with a difference of opinion that each man handled badly.

Choreographing the Dance

Charles had made a unilateral decision that affected Peter's division. When confronted, Charles brushed Peter off, saying, "What do you expect me to do—run around looking for you every time a decision needs to be made? This was just a trivial matter!" (A decidedly one-up stance. Translation: "Oh, pu-leeze! Don't be so petty.") Peter responded, "Trivial! You've screwed things up for two divisions and you call that trivial? We'll be years fixing what you've done. This makes me furious." (Translation: "I'm right, not you, and you should admit it.") Charles replied, "Oh, c'mon, Peter. I don't see why you're so upset. It's not that big a deal." (Translation: "Wrongo, little feller. I'm in charge here.") A shouting match ensued, and Peter stormed out of the office. Over the next few days, they clashed every time they spoke, until Peter finally refused to talk with Charles.

Both Charles and Peter wanted to resolve the conflict, but, like many of us in these situations, didn't know how and were too hurt or angry to try. In a quieter moment, they told me:

CHARLES: "Peter makes a federal case out of everything. He comes in all upset and wants to have it out. I prefer to talk about things rationally. I just want to solve the problem and be done with it, but he wants to talk about how mad he is. I tell him to calm down, that it's not that big a deal. Then he starts yelling and I can't get a word in edgewise.

"The problem now is that he refuses to speak to me. Our two divisions need to work together and he goes through this elaborate process of having one of his managers talk to one of mine, who then brings me the message. It's absurd. Productivity is at a crawl and we both look like idiots."

PETER: "Charles does his own thing and ignores the rest of us. He won't admit that what I do has any value or that I have any expertise, and I'm sick of it. He's demeaning, belittling, and incapable of perceiving that something is a real problem. He goes off making decisions that have ramifications throughout the company and never checks with me about things that are my responsibility. I try to explain that we have to follow certain rules and he'll interrupt with, 'I don't believe in those rules.' I give up. I won't even talk to him anymore. It's not worth the aggravation."

Clearly each vice president bridled at the other's treatment of him. Here's a diagram of their statements:

CHARLES'S PROBLEM:	PETER'S PROBLEM:
Who: Peter	**Who:** Charles
*. . . is doing **what:*** was yelling and demanding his way; now is refusing to speak to Charles	*. . . is doing **what:*** won't acknowledge Peter's worth; won't listen to his views
*. . . **to whom:*** to Charles and his division	*. . . **to whom:*** to Peter and his division
*. . . **how** this behavior is a problem:* can't discuss things rationally; their battle impedes productivity	*. . . **how** this behavior is a problem:* Charles's decisions without input from Peter create problems in the divisions and infuriate Peter.

What they did about their problems with each other made things worse. Charles's main solution was to state in various ways that Peter shouldn't take things so seriously, shouldn't feel so upset. Peter's repeated solution was to tell Charles that he should treat Peter with respect and acknowledge his views.

The more Peter pushed, the more Charles refused. Their solutions created and sustained this dance:

> the more Peter demands that Charles validate his views
>
> the more Charles refuses and trivializes Peter's opinions

To avoid the put-downs, Peter stopped talking to Charles. But that didn't get Charles to cooperate, and it created productivity problems in their divisions.

The Turnaround

Whether they're about business decisions or about who takes out the garbage, conflicts like these are difficult to resolve. Your ego is bruised and you usually aren't inclined to give in or change your tactics *until* the other party meets your demands for deference or validation. But those very demands maintain these conflicts, creating resistance and locking you into the One-upsmanship Dance. As with Charles and Peter, the original disagreement is often forgotten in the struggle for the one-up position.

There's a quick and effective way to untangle these messes, but it takes a bit of courage—the courage to be the first one to change. If you're normal, you want the other guy to come to you first, but, unfortunately, that stance keeps you at his mercy.

OK, you say, you can dredge up an ounce or two of courage, but how do you avoid getting squashed again? Change your dance steps to something unpredictable. You gain control of the situation when the other person doesn't know what to expect from you. It makes that person hesitate and that interrupts the conflict. For instance, look at how predictable Charles and Peter were. Charles knew that Peter would come in yelling, and so had learned to tune him out. Peter knew that Charles had tuned him out and so came in yelling. One of them had to do something new, preferably something that would catch the other by surprise.

Charles told me that he wanted to mend the rift and was willing to swallow some pride, but he wouldn't stand Peter yelling at him again. We began to plan his new strategy. We looked at what Charles did that triggered Peter's outbursts, making Peter's behavior the "logical" response. Charles began to see that his comments ("It's not a big deal . . . It's trivial . . . Just forget it . . . Oh, c'mon, Peter, get over it"), rather than calming Peter, were demeaning and therefore likely to be inflammatory. If he wanted Peter to stop yelling, he'd have to drop the one-up position.

Charles agreed to quit trivializing Peter's opinions and instead show that he took his views seriously. Rather than his usual dismissive put-downs, he would start with something noncommittal like "You have a point. Let me think about it." Or "Tell me more." (Such phrases give you time to think and to avoid your old ineffective reaction.) Also, rather than tell Peter he "had to" do something (a one-up stance), Charles agreed to try something like "I would appreciate it if you would . . ." (a nonconfrontational stance).

But Charles had to break through Peter's silence first. So, in staff meetings, when Peter made a reasonable point, Charles agreed with it and supported him. He began to acknowledge Peter's talents.

Peter, not surprisingly, was suspicious at first. But Charles continued to acknowledge Peter's good ideas and to avoid the belittling remarks of the one-up stance. Peter soon broke his silence, invited Charles out for a drink, and they hammered out an agreement for working together. The conflict that had set the company on edge was over.

Either Side Can Stop a Conflict

But maybe in your situation, you're more like Peter. You're the one who feels put down and at the other person's mercy. And if your Charles has no intention of changing, what can you do?

Either side in a one-upsmanship battle can stop it. As always, look at what you do that may provoke the put-downs. For instance, Peter would have to stop his demands. When you demand that others treat you as superior, you broadcast that you feel inferior. You relinquish your power by demanding something that can be denied you, such as:

- "If you don't get your report to me on time, you'll be sorry."
- "When are you going to think about someone else's needs for a change?"
- "You have got to talk to me before you go changing a decision."
- "What does it take to get a compliment around here?"
- "You never remember my birthday. You'd think just once a year you could think about your wife."

Demands such as these—even when couched as a question—tend to be inflammatory rather than effective. You can't demand cooperation. Well, you can, but it doesn't work. No matter how loudly you roar and how much you bluster, such statements come across as whiny. To return to equal footing, you must take back the power you tossed away. For instance, it is often useful to replace vague demands with specific requests. Rather than yelling "You have got to consider the impact your decisions will have!" (a vague demand), Peter could take a stronger position by saying "I would appreciate it if you would check with me before you revise the safety regulations in the plant" (a specific request). If he really wanted to get Charles's attention and throw him off his stride, he could add, "But of course, I can't make you." With that phrase Peter would state the obvious: that he *can't* force Charles to comply. This disarming statement is so different from Peter's usual attempt to demand compliance that it changes the dance completely.

At first blush, this new solution may seem weak, but in fact it is powerful. Peter's demeanor and words would implicitly establish his equality—leaving Charles no longer in control of that judgment. Assuming equality is more powerful than any demand.

Managers Are Pros at One-Up

Managers can swiftly fall into the one-upsmanship trap. Orin, the manager of a maintenance crew for a public utility, struggled in managing Josh, a capable but haughty young man. During staff meetings, Josh often read the newpaper, made wisecracks during announcements, and argued about work assignments. Orin's "solution" was to take him on, telling him that he had to learn to control himself, arguing with him when he challenged assignments, and occasionally barking at Josh that he had better learn to show some respect.

Josh, having heard such things all his life, would smirk and turn his back or argue with him. Incensed, Orin would carry on about how Josh wouldn't get very far in his career with that attitude, that he would never amount to anything until he learned to show some respect, blah-blah-blah. Of course, Josh just dug in his heels and showed even less respect. Orin's one-up solution perpetuated this dance between them:

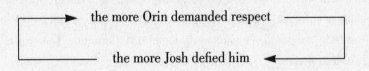

Jumping up and down about his lack of respect (a vague demand at best) got Orin nowhere. Josh was much too practiced at handling that.

The Accidental Fix

Sometimes we happen to do something that stops the conflict, but then we destroy the accord by returning to the same old one-up demands. Orin, not feeling well one day, simply and quietly said, "Josh, I'd appreciate it if I could go through the agenda without interruption and end the meeting early." While the statement itself wasn't dramatic, his shift in approach definitely was. Josh sat quietly and let the meeting proceed. Orin had accidentally found an effective approach. But then, instead of quitting while he was ahead, Orin said, "See, Josh? Isn't this better? If you'd only act like this more often . . ."

At that point, Josh mumbled, "Oh, put a sock in it."

Orin came back with, "Young man, if you'd do something about that attitude of yours, you just might have a chance of turning into a decent human being."

The battle was on again—at Orin's instigation.

It is so tempting to try for the last word. Your tongue just itches to declare yourself the victor. ("Thanks for the flowers, honey. They're lovely. If you'd only remembered our other anniversaries . . .") Unfortunately, when you scratch that itch, you again demand acknowledgment of your superiority and you're back to where you started—losing.

I think we hand back our victory for one reason: We don't notice that we've won. And we don't notice our success for one reason—we forget what problem we were trying to solve. Orin wanted "respect"—a vague and general demand. The actual problem was:

- *Who:* Josh
- *is doing what:* interrupting staff meetings with wisecracks and arguments

- *to whom:* to Orin and other employees
- *how this behavior is a problem:* the meetings drag on and people get frustrated.

Orin needed Josh to listen and contribute productively, or at least be quiet. Haranguing him to show respect was off the mark and left Orin unclear about what "showing respect" would look like. So when Orin's quiet and specific request succeeded where vague demands hadn't, he again demanded explicit deference instead of silently celebrating the implicit deference Josh had already given.

In Summary

In most conflicts it's best to not take a rigid, confrontational stance. The one-up position will usually trigger a similar stance from others as they try to get even, either actively or subtly. While tempting, this reaction prolongs the conflict, obscures the problem that needs solving, and leaves residual resentment festering. A more nonconfrontational stance avoids these hazards and can be much more effective.

NINE

Solution by Evasion: Using the Indirect Approach

Sometimes we hesitate to address the irritants in our lives—perhaps the friend who complains too much, or the co-worker who gossips nonstop, or the boss who skewers with barbed humor. Rather than acting, we tell ourselves that we can tolerate their quirks. We hesitate to do anything for a host of reasons:

- What if our co-worker holds a grudge?
- What if our friend pouts for weeks?
- What if they can't—or won't—change?
- What if they think (worse yet, say) that we're petty or too sensitive?
- What if they turn on us and point out all the annoying, self-serving, exasperating things *we* do, mentioning in passing how magnanimous they've always been in overlooking our shortcomings?
- What if all of the above happen?

Then what? We'd wish we'd never said anything, that we could take everything back: "Gosh, I didn't mean to make you feel bad . . . It's not really that big a deal . . . I shouldn't have brought it up . . . Forget I ever said anything—here, let me pay for lunch."

Because of these real or imagined dangers, we often don't address the issue directly. But with each repetition, their habits get harder to bear. Over time their habits become as unbearable as that gopher in your rose garden.

The "do-nothing" stance rarely works because:

> the more we tell ourselves to "just ignore it"
>
> the stronger our resentment grows

And because our resentment keeps growing, we're likely to poke and prod in indirect ways: 1) we hint about what they should change; 2) we make a general comment to everyone instead of speaking directly to the offending individual; 3) we speak in generalities about the problem; or 4) we avoid the person entirely.

These indirect nudges can get your friend, co-worker, or boss to change but only when they are receptive, can read between the lines, and are willing to make the hinted-at changes. At other times, subtlety doesn't work and becomes part of the problem. Here's how these ineffective approaches play out.

1. HINTING AND HOPING

Let's say that your co-worker comes in late most days, then plays video games while you wait impatiently for her project.

But instead of telling her directly what bugs you, you hint about the problem ("Wouldn't it be something if the project was on time for a change"), or joke about what bothers you ("Late again! You must hold the world's record for finding traffic jams!"). You make vague suggestions ("Maybe we should get together sometime and see if we can speed things up"), and even try sarcasm ("So, what's your score for solitaire *today*?"). Sometimes you nudge nonverbally: You roll your eyes or frown when your co-worker explains why she's late again; you sigh loudly when you see solitaire on her screen. You try everything—everything except telling her in a straightforward way what the problem is. Your frustration builds as, time after time, you must scramble to finish a project on time after she finally hands it over.

You wonder why she doesn't change since it's so obvious what's bothering you. But some people are oblivious to subtlety. Your co-worker may only pick up on the fact that you're unhappy but not realize why. Or she may know what's bothering you but see it as insignificant, so feels no urgency to change. Or she may ignore you because, as one project manager put it, "Yeah, I know what Don wants me to change, but if he doesn't have the guts to say so directly, screw him!"

Many people take a hint, but if your hinting hasn't worked yet, your co-worker isn't one of them. If you want her to change, you'll need to give up the indirect approach and try something different, like being direct. For instance, you could tell her directly the impact of her delayed project: late nights and weekend work for your team. Be careful to stick to the facts and describe the specific problem her specific behavior causes. Resist the urge to call her all the names you've saved up or to dump on her all the resentment you've accumulated. That will only create resistance or spark retaliation. And don't accept a vague promise to "try harder," but work with her to outline a specific action plan. In a surprising number of situations, your shift to this direct approach will get you the change you've wanted. When the indirect approach has been your ineffective remedy, then the direct approach is worth a try. If it doesn't happen to work, try one of the other options you've already read about, like setting up consequences. But don't keep hinting when it clearly isn't working. It only keeps you in the dance.

Another form of hinting that rarely works is the lob.

2. THE LOB: DIRECTING THE MESSAGE TO THE GROUP

- "It has come to my attention that some people aren't taking responsibility for the mistakes in their units . . ."
- "We all need to keep in mind that being late for meetings wastes time and that everyone's time is important . . ."
- "If everyone would clean up their own messes in the lunchroom and brew a new pot of coffee when they take the last cup, we'd eliminate a lot of grumbling around here."

These are examples of the second indirect method: lobbing a request for change at everyone and hoping it strikes the guilty party. Sometimes this works, but more often your target doesn't recognize that the message had his name on it. Or he may decide that everyone must be making the same mistake, so there's no need to change. This solution could be worth a try once, but if it doesn't produce results quickly, drop it and switch to a more one-on-one direct method.

3. "BE MORE . . .": GENERALITIES AREN'T SOLUTIONS

Teresa, a sales manager in a Wichita, Kansas, life insurance agency, advised her young sales representative to "be more professional." Teresa meant that she should stop rambling on and on in staff meetings and should help solve business problems instead of blaming others. But the young saleswoman took "be more professional" to mean *look* more professional. She bought conservative business suits and had her hair professionally styled, but continued to babble on in staff meetings in the same oblivious manner.

This is the third indirect approach that often fails—speaking in generalities. Like Teresa, you may think that you've been perfectly clear about what someone needs to change, only to find yourself disappointed with the results. But rather than being clear, you may have said something like:

- "Be more productive."
- "Show some initiative."
- "Keep me informed."
- "Be a team player."
- "Manage your people better."
- "Stop being such a _____ [fill in the blank]."

Such statements don't spell out what change you expect. If you ask your administrative assistant to "show some initiative," what, exactly, do you mean? Should he solve more problems on his own? Work more actively to promote his career? Speak up in meetings? Take on new projects? Challenge the status quo?

Your assistant hasn't been privy to your private thoughts, so he's likely to miss the meaning of your terse directive. He hasn't been inside your head and so won't know that you've been wondering how to change his timidity in meetings, for instance. But after you've thought about the problem long enough, it's easy to assume your assistant must be aware of it too. When you finally tell him to "show some initiative," your meaning is clear—but probably only to you.

You could get lucky: Some people read between the lines. But if your assistant doesn't, then you have to try something different. If you've only tried indirect methods, then the simple, direct approach is certainly worth a try. As a consultant, I'm always surprised by how seldom people use it and how often it works.

The Culture Counts

Some corporate cultures encourage indirectness. It may be the preferred style of the chief executive, who then rewards it in others. Or perhaps your manager or human resources group, concerned about legal retribution, cautions you not to confront someone or to impose consequences. But whatever the organizational reason, if the indirect approach has failed, continued indirectness will only bring continued failure. If you balk at or are constrained from using the direct method, then try something else—perhaps techniques from the previous chapters. Many of them (like encouraging someone not to change) might work in this situation.

A Few Comments About the Direct Approach

This is not what I mean by the direct approach: "Look. I'm telling you this for your own good because you're ruining your career. No one wants to work with you or to be on your team. You drive people nuts and . . ." The guy on the receiving end is likely to feel defensive, hurt, angry, or all three. And you won't like the response you get. There's an art to the successful direct approach. Here are a few tips:

Stick to the facts. Tell the other person specifically what the problem is (who is doing what to whom) without judgments or labels. Explain how these actions affect you or others (how this behavior is a problem). Be specific; for example, "when your work gets to me two weeks late" versus "when you goof off and take your sweet time about getting serious around here." "You need to be more considerate of others" is vague, whereas, "You need to keep your voice down when you're on the phone in your cubicle" is specific.

Consider timing. If your colleague is rushing to leave the office early on Friday, you're not likely to find her receptive to your message late that afternoon, for example.

Consider the staging. Your place or hers? Will the other person be more willing to listen if you meet in her office or in yours? Perhaps neutral territory would be best.

Be prepared for the other person's surprise. Don't assume he'll be aware of the problem you're bringing up. Work with him to understand what you're saying—give examples, listen to his response, and offer to help figure out what to do to fix the problem. If he acts defensive,

hurt, or angry, actively try to understand his view and acknowledge his feelings, but bring the conversation back
to the main problem if it strays. Then work with him to
design a plan for change.

The test of any solution is whether or not it gets someone to
change. Many people respond to hints, but if your problem person doesn't, then you need to drop the indirect approach and do
something different. Be direct.

4. AVOIDING THE PROBLEM—AND THE SOLUTION

The fourth indirect method is avoidance. It isn't actually a
way to get someone to change but is rather a way to dodge the
issue. Sometimes it's the rational thing to do. If you can avoid
working for the whiner in Marketing or the screamer in Sales, do
it. But if you're already stuck with them, avoiding the issue
doesn't always work.

For example, Jan and Don, partners in a small greeting-card
business, jointly managed their fifteen employees. While Jan
worked well with everyone, Don was notorious for his frequent
blow-ups and condescending tone. Jan worried that this would
affect productivity, but the work was getting done, and on the
whole, business was good. Not wanting to trigger his explosive
temper, she put off saying anything to Don and instead pleaded
with their employees to have patience.

When an important project floundered, Jan found a face-
saving way to relieve Don of the lead role. She hoped that Don
would notice how she handled the employees and learn from her

example. No such luck. Don continued to push his own ideas, explode in anger, and pontificate.

When several workers threatened to quit, Jan finally admitted she had to do something. By then she had a long list of concerns and resentments and felt nervous about dumping them on him. So before she confronted him, she defined the problem clearly, whittling her list down to these key issues:

- **Who:** Don
- *is doing* **what:** talking to the employees in a condescending tone; exploding in anger; pushing his own ideas and not listening to others
- **to whom:** the employees who work on his projects
- **how** *this behavior is a problem:* employees are demoralized and reluctant to work on his projects; creativity is stifled; employees spend time grumbling rather than working

Then Jan wrote down specific examples of troublesome things he'd said and done. Only then did she sit down and talk with him. To Jan's relief, Don listened. To her surprise, he acknowledged that he was doing a poor job with the employees and admitted that it bothered him. He was willing to work on the problem but didn't know what to do. When Jan offered to coach him, he readily accepted.

It took effort on Don's part to change his management style and on Jan's part to give feedback and, later, encouragement, but Don was willing and able—once the issue was out in the open. While he never worked as comfortably with the employees as Jan, he improved significantly.

Drifting into Avoidance

Avoidance is easy to drift into as each day you postpone action for just "one more day." This strategy can work—*if* you harbor no resentments and there are no troublesome consequences mounting. But resentments and consequences tend to grow. You may find yourself more and more riled by someone's annoying actions, so that when you finally speak out, you're likely to use words dripping with judgment or emotion. And with those words you're more likely to produce the very emotional response you'd dreaded, one you might have avoided if you'd dealt with things earlier.

Even high-risk directness—like confronting the boss—can work out well. For example, Tim, the founder and president of a computer start-up company, was a young man of formidable intelligence and vision. Unfortunately, he demonstrated his utter disdain for "mere mortals" by frequent sarcasm, outbursts, and brutal cross-examinations. No one would confront him, although many working hours were lost in grousing, licking wounds, and searching for the courage to face him. Finally, his staff, through a survey-feedback process, was able to tell him about the impact of his management style—creative people leaving the company, those remaining feeling demoralized, and chronic low productivity. After a couple of weeks of protesting and then of soul-searching, Tim agreed that his style was a significant problem. However, since he felt unsure that he could change—certainly not in time to help the young, struggling company—he chose to step down as president and return to the lab where he (and consequently the rest of the company) was much happier and more productive.

In Summary

There is nothing inherently wrong with the indirect approaches—hinting, lobbing, speaking in generalities, or avoiding. If they produce the change you need, you've saved yourself a lot of time and trouble. But when they don't work, don't waste your time trying them over and over. You'll only let the situation (and your mood) get worse. Move on to a different strategy.

When You Are
Your Problem:
Trying to Conquer Fear
with Endless Preparation

Some irritating problems don't need anyone else's involvement. You perform the entire dance by yourself. For example, without a partner you can successfully execute the Procrastination-Guilt Ballet, the Worrywart Hip-Hop, the Late-Again-Oh-No Tap Dance, and the Temper Tantrum Stomp. In these situations, you're the one bothered by your behavior, you're the one who lectures you to quit it, and you're the one who keeps on doing it anyway. While others may join in—perhaps by giving you advice from the sidelines that echoes your own pep talks—for the most part, it is you against yourself.

You get into trouble when trying to change yourself the same way you do when trying to change someone else. You pick a strategy that doesn't happen to work, and when it fails, you repeat that strategy again and again. Kent, a self-employed consultant specializing in management development training, is a good example.

Fear and Loathing

Kent had built a small and loyal clientele through referrals from colleagues and friends. But to survive financially he needed additional clients. He knew he had to market more aggressively, but hated making cold sales calls. He wasn't good at them and dreaded the rejections. He had to get past this fear, so he took sales classes, read sales and communications books, asked salespeople for advice, and wrote sales pitches that he rehearsed endlessly. He did everything except make an actual call.

No matter how much he prepared, he never felt ready. The more he postponed cold calls, the stronger his anxiety became. The stronger his anxiety, the less he felt prepared. The less he felt prepared, the more books he read and advice he sought.

Anyone can get caught, like Kent, in the "endless preparation" cycle. Your efforts revolve around trying to extinguish all apprehension *before* undertaking your feared task. You want to do the dreaded task perfectly, to feel sure you've mastered it before you try it. You rehearse a hundred times how you'll ask for that raise, but worry that you haven't found just the right words—yet. Or you agonize every night at dinner about the best way to confront an incessant talker on your team, until your spouse won't listen to another word. Or you practice over and over how to present your brainstorm for increasing market share, trying to anticipate every possible objection until, wound up in knots, you decide maybe it was just a braindrizzle after all.

You tell yourself over and over that you're not ready because, "I should not feel afraid or unsure." But that erroneous thought is what keeps you vapor-locked. It's impossible to know how you'll perform before you've tried something, so naturally you will feel some—maybe considerable—anxiety. More preparation won't eliminate your anxiety. It can't. At this stage only action can.

What—Me Worry?

But if taking action were easy, you'd have done it already. While you tackle other tasks in your life by doing them imperfectly and learning from trial and error, you don't try that with the task you fear. You've built up such performance anxiety that a mistake seems a punishable crime, not a simple and inevitable step in the learning process.

So you need to take an unusual step to get yourself going, and that is to fail *on purpose:* A tiny, meaningless failure will do nicely.

For example, Kent finally decided to face his nervousness about cold sales calls and get a rejection under his belt. From his client list he chose an engineering manager renowned for refusing management training. Assured of a rejection, and therefore with nothing to lose, Kent made the call. Predictably, he got turned down in short order. While rejection wasn't enjoyable, Kent found that he actually felt relief for having made a move. He used his experience to improve his sales pitch, which he tried again with another predictable rejector. After a very short time, Kent tried a genuine cold call, doing it with fear and trepidation, but doing it nevertheless. Then he did another and another, and soon cold calls became a normal part of his work week.

It is taking action that breaks up this dance, taking action that should strive for imperfection. This is effective even when you act reluctantly. Once you've made a move, the worst is over. This is what Sharon, a forty-two-year-old sales manager for an Oakland, California, computer company discovered.

A Realistic Fear

On October 17, 1989, Sharon was driving home across the San Francisco Bay Bridge. Suddenly she had trouble controlling her car. In her rearview mirror she saw the section of bridge she'd just driven over buckle and drop out of sight in a cloud of dust. The bridge continued to buck and shake as the Loma Prieta earthquake struck northern California. Terrified that the whole bridge would collapse, she raced across the bridge at eighty miles an hour, not stopping until she arrived home safe but hysterical.

During the month the bridge was out of commission, her daily commute around the bay cost her two extra hours each way. In spite of that, when the repaired bridge reopened, Sharon couldn't make herself use it. She was terrified. But rather than realizing that her fear was normal and understandable, she felt she should "just get over it." She told herself over and over: "I'm being foolish. I shouldn't be afraid. They wouldn't let people use the bridge if it wasn't safe. Besides, what are the chances that another quake will hit when I'm on the bridge? It's a once-in-a-lifetime horror." But her fear persisted, as did her awful commute.

Sharon kept trying to talk herself out of her fear before taking action. As could be expected, telling someone—even yourself—to not feel something doesn't work. It usually makes the feeling more intense. You may remember this from the last time your spouse came home enraged at the stupid, insensitive, mean, crass thing her boss had done that day, and you said, "Oh, honey, you shouldn't let him get to you like this. You shouldn't get so upset. Just let it go." You knew you were in trouble when she responded: "Not be upset? You weren't there! You don't understand just how bad this guy is. Why, he . . ." Your wife then was not only mad at her insensitive boss, but at her "insensitive" husband. And she probably spent the next several minutes trying to prove to you that her feelings were justified. Deny feelings and they intensify.

And so it happened with Sharon:

the more she told herself she shouldn't be afraid

the more her fear persisted

Sharon needed to make a move, even a small move, in spite of her fear. For instance, she could have gone and stood at the edge of a different bridge, like the Golden Gate, walked on it a short distance, and then retreated. She could have ridden across in someone else's car, trembling in the backseat. Or, more simply, she could have told herself that her fear was reasonable. Any actions like these would have broken the cycle.

For Sharon, the problem was solved abruptly. One evening in heavy rush-hour traffic she couldn't change lanes and got trapped in the bridge access lane. Unable to stop, she was forced onto the bridge. She drove across, shaking the whole way—especially when she had to cross the recognizably replaced section of bridge. The next day she took the bridge to work instead of commuting around the bay, and every day after that. After several trips across the bridge, her fear dissipated. Action in spite of fear (even though not by her own choice) resolved the problem.

If you find yourself postponing a feared action until you feel completely prepared or until you talk yourself out of your "unreasonable" feelings, stop. Choose instead some small action that you can afford to fail at and therefore learn from. Do it in spite of your anxiety because your behavior must change first; your feelings will change later. The following exercise will help you get started.

TO TAKE ACTION WHEN FEARFUL

1. Acknowledge that you can't talk yourself out of your feelings. They don't respond to logical persuasion.
2. Ask yourself: What's the smallest step in the right direction that I can take? Or, better yet, ask: What small step can I purposefully fail at to learn its lesson?
3. Try it.

In Summary—Just Do Something Different

People often fail to get themselves or others to change because they have employed the ineffective "solutions" you've seen in this chapter and in the previous ones. But more than remembering these particular solutions, it's important to remember that *any* tack you're pursuing that is not producing results is contributing to the problem, not solving it. Figure out what you're doing over and over that isn't working. Then, at the very least, stop doing "more of the same." *Do something different.*

Next you'll learn a number of ways to devise the "something different" you need to do.

SECTION III:

Hunting Down
New Solutions

You've seen a number of solutions my clients have used successfully, so you may already have found the answer for your own predicament. But perhaps your situation is different from theirs or you'd like to see more options before choosing your new game plan.

Chapter eleven is a smorgasbord of techniques to help you figure out what your "something different" will be. Pick the ones that fit your fancy—and your situation. Then chapters twelve through fifteen will help you troubleshoot and implement your plan, and show you how to learn this process quickly.

Changing the Dance: Doing the Opposite, the Unexpected, the Outrageous, and the Ordinary

It's one thing to diagnose the problem, Watson.
It's quite another to resolve it.
—SHERLOCK HOLMES

It's time to pick your new strategy for getting your boss to stop nitpicking or your colleague to stop procrastinating or your spouse to start helping with the housework (or yard work). So how do you make sure that your new solution is appreciably different from what you were doing before, that you don't fall back into the "more of the same" trap?

You've done the groundwork already. In step one—**What is the primary problem?**—you figured out the most important issue to tackle and spelled out the facts:

> **Who** is doing
>> **what** that presents a problem,
>>> **to whom,** and
>>>> **how** is this behavior a problem?

So you've already made sure you will get the most mileage from your efforts by focusing on your central issue.

In step two—**What have you been doing about your problem so far?**—you identified the basic statement you've been unsuccessfully repeating about what someone should or should not do, or should or should not feel. So you know what to avoid: any solution that again conveys that same message.

With your work from steps one and two to guide you, you're ready for step three: **What do you need to do instead?** It's time to pick the solution that will be significantly different from your ineffective one and finally get you the change you're after.

Sometimes your new solution will require you to make a dramatic shift in strategy. In other situations you will only need to take a small sidestep. In this chapter you'll see examples of both. But whether your shift is big or small, *anything different* is better than what you've been doing. A number of solutions will work as long as you avoid the one that hasn't.

A Word of Encouragement—and Warning

The following methods have all been used successfully by my clients, friends, and colleagues to figure out how to stop doing "more of the same" and finally get someone to change their irritating behavior. (As with all examples in this book, their identities have been disguised.) Some of these solutions are simple and straightforward and will fit the average corporate culture (or the average family). Others may seem outrageous—and they are. They fit the personalities of my clients or friends and they worked well, but you may blanch at the thought of doing them yourself. But don't summarily toss out these unusual methods. If you stay only in your comfort zone, you risk staying with the solution that doesn't work. Toy with ways to tone down the unusual solutions, to adapt them to your own style. Use them to stretch your thinking and challenge yourself about what you could do that would be quite different from what you already know doesn't work.

So grab your notes about what specifically you want to change and what solution you need to avoid. Then use one of the following methods to choose your new game plan. As with any problem-solving process, first choose your new strategy—what you will do differently. Then work on your implementation plan —how you'll do it.

1. DO THE FOSBURY FLOP

In 1968 Dick Fosbury made track and field history by doing things backward. During training, Dick wasn't satisfied with his performance in the high jump so he decided to try something different—quite different. Athletes normally cleared the high bar by rolling over it facedown. But when Dick ran to the bar he turned and, arching his back, launched himself over the bar belly up, kicking his legs up and over last, landing with a splat on the other side. This unorthodox style brought him considerable scorn until the 1968 Olympic Games where he won a gold medal with a jump of 7 feet, 4 1/2 inches. Now it is rare to find a high jumper who doesn't do the "Fosbury Flop."

Your ideal solution, like Dick Fosbury's, may be 180 degrees different from what you've been trying. One of the easiest ways to find a successful strategy is to start with the opposite of your current one.

For instance, Patricia, a ranger with the National Park Service, was at a loss about how to deal with Roger, the park's resource manager. No matter what idea anyone came up with, he could find a reason why it wouldn't work. He was an intelligent man and his comments usually had merit; but after a couple of hours of listening to his "that'll never work" mantra, the team slumped despondently. Patricia couldn't stand the situation anymore, but nothing she'd tried had helped. Frustrated, she knew she needed to try something new.

First, she defined the problem:

- *Who:* Roger
- *is doing what:* constantly pointing out what's wrong with every idea
- *to whom this is a problem:* Patricia and the rest of the team
- *how this is a problem:* his negativity destroys the team's creativity and diminishes its ability to solve problems and to plan successfully

Then Patricia reviewed her futile efforts. She had:

- asked Roger privately to stop being so negative
- warned him about the damage to his career if he didn't change his behavior
- cautioned him that others had reasonable ideas, and that he should give the team a chance to explore them
- tried to use formal brainstorming rules that inhibited criticism (but he ignored them)
- finally yelled at him to be quiet

Staring at the list, Patricia realized that she had asked, reasoned, threatened, and yelled, but the theme was always the same: "You should stop being negative." Regardless of how she delivered that message, it obviously wasn't working. Roger had actually become even more negative, and her repeated message to him had now become her part in the dance:

the more Patricia told him to stop being negative

the more negative Roger became

She knew she could begin formal disciplinary steps, but she dreaded the paperwork and the time that would require. She decided to try something else first. To come up with a new solution, Patricia figured that she'd use the exact opposite of the ineffective one, which would be to tell Roger he should be even more negative, strange as this might sound. The idea intrigued her as she thought about how it would surprise him. Patricia then worked out how to execute this 180-degree turn—a plan that just might get Roger to think twice before opening his mouth. She tried out her idea at the next staff meeting.

After stating the meeting's agenda Patricia made an announcement: "I've been thinking about our meetings, and I've realized that I have made a mistake. I've been trying to smother critical comments that are really to our benefit. We should be thinking carefully about what might go wrong with any plans we contemplate. It could save us time and money in the long run. So I'm appointing you, Roger, to be the critic in these meetings. You're good at it, and we need criticism. To make up for my previous attempts to douse your views, I'd prefer you to make an error toward being too critical. So please make criticisms even when you aren't sure if it's that important a point. I want you to be critical—more so than before." Roger mumbled something about that being a rotten idea and Patricia said, "Thank you. That's exactly what I had in mind."

As the meeting progressed, she didn't wait passively for Roger to sidetrack the team with his negativity. She stayed ahead of him and in charge by actively asking Roger for his opinions about what was wrong with a particular plan or what problems he thought the team was ignoring. Roger was unusually quiet during the meeting, except to respond to Patricia's questions with uncharacteristic comments like "I think the idea's OK" or "It might work." Over the next few months, Roger began to offer more constructive ideas at meetings, in his grumbling sort of way. When he was negative, the team—with Patricia's guidance—began to treat his comments as useful. The team lost its despondency and became quite creative.

Undoing What You've Done

How does such a seemingly crazy tactic work? When you change significantly what you're doing, you no longer provide a cue for the same troublesome behavior to begin. Your difficult person can't continue the same old routine because you've thrown off his rhythm. You are undoing what your ineffective solution did that turned the initial problem (a critical employee) into a recurring one (a struggle between manager and employee). Patricia's Fosbury Flop—encouraging even more negativity— undid the power struggle.

But the opposite of an ineffective solution is *not* to stop doing it. That rarely works. Suppose Patricia had decided to stop lecturing Roger about his critical style and instead said nothing. Silence is not the opposite solution. Roger would likely not perceive any real change in her behavior—believing her still to be annoyed, just brooding silently at the moment. Nor would Patricia be doing anything active to solve the problem. Her frustration would likely build as Roger continued to criticize everything until Patricia finally exploded. In the end, nothing would have changed, except possibly the decibel level of their discussions.

A change of manner is not a change of strategy, either. For instance, when Patricia switched from reasoning with Roger that he was hurting his career and instead yelled at him and threatened to demote him, she hadn't changed strategy. She had simply tried another method to push the same basic strategy: "You should stop being negative."

How to Implement the Fosbury Flop Solution

There are many ways to implement the Fosbury Flop solution. In earlier examples you've read about a number of successful 180-degree turns:

- "You should stick to the schedule," said Kevin ineffectually to his co-trainer Carol. The opposite was "You should not stick to the schedule." He implemented that by telling her to take all the time she wanted, that he wanted to emulate her relaxed style, and to prove it, he stopped policing her or reminding her. (See page 93.)
- "You should treat people better," Kelly repeatedly told her vice-president, Jake. When Kelly instead assigned a prized project to another employee, telling Jake she had done so because "it would be a burden for Jake to control himself," her implicit message was a 180-degree

turn: "I'm not asking you to treat people better." (See page 100.)

- "You should stop belittling me in staff meetings," Jeanette said, trying to get through to her abrasive peer Gwen. She succeeded in getting Gwen to stop when she turned 180 degrees and said, "Please continue to belittle my work; our boss treats me better when you do." (See page 102.)

So the first method for finding a successful way to get someone to change is to:

> Think in terms of the exact opposite.

This exercise will show you your Fosbury Flop.

TO FIND THE OPPOSITE

1. Again refer to the problem you've been analyzing in the previous exercises. Write a concise sentence that captures the basic message or theme of your repeated ineffective solution.

EXAMPLES
Patricia's statement to Roger: "You should not be negative."
Kevin's statement to his co-trainer: "You should stick to the schedule."

2. Change your theme sentence by simply adding a "not" (or eliminating the "not" if one is there). This is the opposite solution and becomes your new strategy.

EXAMPLES
Patricia's solution turned into "You *should* be negative."
Kevin's turned into "You should *not* stick to the schedule."

3. Now brainstorm ways to implement this new strategy. Then pick from your list what you will say and/or do to deliver your new message.

EXAMPLES
Patricia: "I've realized that critical comments benefit our planning efforts and I've decided to appoint you our critic."
Kevin: "Take all the time you want with your training. I want to learn to lecture in as relaxed a fashion as you do."

Here's a second method for finding a workable solution and getting the change you want.

2. START SMALL

Your new solution doesn't have to be dramatic. As long as your actions are very different from what you were doing before, a small change can turn things around. Two vice presidents had spent years trading insults, making staff meetings a battlefield. While they never became friends, they did begin working reasonably well together when one of them changed one simple thing. Instead of disagreeing with every comment the other made, he began to say "You have an interesting point. Let me think about it" or "Tell me more." Without agreeing or disagreeing, he gave himself time to consider the other's point, and let the other man know that that was what he was doing. While small, the change was enough to interrupt the usual exchange of insults. It started the two of them down the road to a more productive working relationship.

Give Small a Chance

It doesn't hurt to start small as long as you choose a different tack from your unsuccessful one. You can always adjust later, if necessary.

Clients of mine found these small changes enough to remedy the particular troublesome situations they faced:

- In the face of constant criticism, silently taking notes of what was being said, then reading those notes back—instead of actively defending each critical point.
- Making statements ("Unless it creates a problem for you, I'm going to do X") instead of asking permission ("Would it be OK if I did X?").
- Giving a specific compliment to the other party in a conflict ("I like the way you presented your report—your lineup of facts made it easy to follow") instead of continuing the silent treatment or harsh rebuttal.
- Excusing oneself for a few minutes—in the midst of a heated discussion—to go to the bathroom instead of escalating the argument.

- Holding back for thirty minutes before rushing in to fix a problem for someone else.

To start small:

> Think in terms of changes that are small
> but very different from the same old solution.

Whether you're choosing small changes or dramatic ones, it can help to pick a solution that blocks your return to old habits.

3. SET UP A ROADBLOCK

In the proverbial heat of battle, you will be drawn to your old familiar solution, not because it works but because repetition has made it almost a knee-jerk reaction. So sometimes you need to pick a new solution that will act as a roadblock between you and your old ineffective response.

Philip, a marketing manager with a young team, asked me to help him fix his team's "lack of creativity." When we explored the problem further, Philip described his habit of constantly critiquing his staff's ideas, which he saw as a way of teaching them. But as we talked, he began to see that his criticism contributed to the problem and locked him in this circular pattern:

```
 ┌──────▶  the more Philip tried to educate with criticism ──────┐
 │                                                                │
 └──────────  the fewer creative ideas came from the staff  ◀─────┘
```

Philip knew that he'd have trouble changing his critical style. His quick mind and his drive to get things done made him impatient with his staff's slower pace. But he wanted to change, so we installed two roadblocks to make it harder for him to slip back into his critical and demotivating style.

First, during meetings Philip wrote his staff's ideas down on a flip chart before reacting. Since it is difficult to write and speak simultaneously, this gave him time to consider their ideas and to remember his resolve not to criticize everything. He then would ask for more ideas, still without critiquing. Then the staff and Philip together culled and tailored the resulting list of ideas into something usable.

Second, for the inevitable times—especially at first—when Philip would forget and slip back into criticism, the staff devised a "reminder" that functioned as the second roadblock. If Philip criticized an idea, the whole staff would sit up stiffly, silently stare straight ahead, and fold their hands in front of them (like good little schoolchildren). At the absurdity of this scene Philip couldn't help but laugh and would then return to listening and recording their ideas. The team could have devised a number of other ways to react to Philip, but this solution came to mind and fit the nature of the group. It let them "confront" their manager with humor.

Over time the staff grew in courage and learned to push back appropriately, and Philip figured out when criticism helped and when it hindered. As the staff's creativity increased, Philip noticed how much they had to offer. The staff also learned the value of Philip's experience and viewpoint and often actively sought his critique.

It's always useful, as you consider a new solution, to design one that interferes with regressing to your old ways. It doesn't need to be elaborate. The age-old wisdom of counting to ten might be all it takes to get control of your fiery temper, for instance. (OK, maybe you need to count to twenty.) Or if you tend to overcommit yourself, you could make it a rule to say "Let me get back to you on that" whenever you're asked to do something. So as you choose a new strategy:

> Pick a new solution that interferes with repeating your old solution.

But maybe you don't need to come up with a new strategy after all. Here's another way to get the change you're after.

4. NOTICE WHEN IT ISN'T HAPPENING

Consider the possibility that you already know how to get someone to change. Steve de Shazer, a therapist and the author of many books, including *Keys to Solutions in Brief Therapy*, notes that there are times when frustrating behavior doesn't occur even though the circumstances were ripe for it. For once, your manager didn't blow up or didn't second-guess your decision. Somehow you handled the situation differently—and successfully. But you may not have noticed this. People tend to overlook what *didn't* happen and therefore miss important clues. Like Sherlock Holmes who once solved a mystery by noticing that the dog hadn't barked when it should have, you may find the answer to your problem by noting when your problem doesn't occur.

If your manager didn't run her number on you as usual, it's

probable that you did something that prevented it. So you've already gotten your manager to change—you just need to figure out what you did and do it again. But you may have completely overlooked your momentary success because: 1) you didn't notice that the problem could have occurred but didn't; or 2) you didn't give yourself credit for actively preventing the problem, instead chalking it up to luck; or 3) you noticed your success but wrote it off as a fluke: "Well, it's because my manager was in a rare good mood today."

To discover what worked, ask yourself these questions:

1. What is happening when the problem *isn't* happening—what are you doing then?
2. How can you do that some more?

For example, think about how you handle problems when you feel good about yourself. You trot into the office full of energy and when you see the office grump lumbering toward your desk, you sing out, "Not today, Halley. Only good news today!" And Halley nods glumly and wanders off in search of some other victim. But on the days you feel tired or distracted, you don't use your perfectly workable solution to take charge of the situation. You see Halley headed your way and you hunker down to endure. You already know how to handle Halley—you just forget to use what you know.

My mother was an intelligent and wonderful woman with one typical parental trait. She loved to impose unending advice on her grown children. Years ago, I can remember her telephoning to see how I was doing. Well, I didn't want to tell her about my latest worry because I didn't want her usual motherly advice. But, as intuitive as ever, she soon asked, "What's wrong?" and I felt caught. Suddenly I heard myself say something I'd never said before: "Mom, I'd like to tell you, but I don't want advice yet. I just need you to listen. OK?" She agreed. She then completely surprised me by becoming the perfect sounding board, playing back what she heard me saying so I could sort the problem out for myself. She didn't offer a single word of advice. We had a wonderful conversation that day and many more over the years—when I remembered to use my new antidote for her unsolicited advice.

So another way to find out how to get someone to change is to:

> Notice what you did or said differently
> when the usual problem didn't occur.

Use the following exercise to discover the solution you already know.

TO DISCOVER THE SOLUTION YOU ALREADY KNOW

1. Recall times when the troublesome behavior didn't occur, or occurred in a more tolerable form. What was different about those occasions? Note, for instance, differences in time, location, who was involved . . .
2. Think about what you did or said that was different. Note what was different about your tone of voice, your actions, your words (or lack of words), your demeanor . . .
3. Figure out how you can repeat your success. Don't write it off as a fluke, but push yourself to remember what you did

differently, or figure out how to re-create the circum-stances that caused the "fluke."

Another way to find a workable strategy is to borrow one.

5. FIND SOMEONE WITH IMMUNITY

You may not know how to get someone to change, but you may know someone who does. An abrasive manager may not be abrasive to everyone or a lazy employee may work hard for one particular team leader. Observing how others successfully han-dle your nemesis can often be illuminating.

A teacher who worked in the same high school as my hus-band was struggling with an aggravating and arrogant student. She dreaded the days Alan showed up for class. Finally she asked my husband—who had little trouble with Alan—how he handled him. "Well, he's a tough one, that's for sure," he said. "But I happened upon something that works. One day I was a couple of minutes late to class and as I walked in, Alan hollered, 'Hey, Bucko, you're late!' I pointed at him and said, 'That's MIS-TER Bucko to you.' Alan laughed and settled down to work. I've found that he responds very well to the humorous or the low-key approach. If you take him on or act superior, he's impossible."

Don't hesitate to ask someone how he handles the person who's driving you crazy. There's nothing wrong with borrowing good ideas.

> Find out how someone else successfully handles the troublesome behavior that you're struggling with.

A sixth way to change your strategy is to become unpredictable.

6. DO THE UNEXPECTED

To find a workable solution, answer these questions: What would make you less predictable? What would be an unexpected, uncharacteristic thing for you to do?

Doing the unexpected can mean stating something so obvious that people are at a loss as to how to respond. In the book *Change: Principles of Problem Formation and Problem Resolution*, there is a story about a police officer who pulled over a speeder. As he wrote up the ticket, he noticed that an unfriendly crowd was beginning to gather around him. By the time he had handed the speeder his citation, the crowd was moving ominously closer and the sergeant was not sure if he would get back to his patrol car safely. It then occurred to him to announce in a loud voice: 'You have just witnessed the issuance of a traffic ticket by a member of your Oakland Police Department.' And while the crowd digested this perplexingly obvious statement, he walked to his patrol car, got in, and drove off.

The police officer had to think quickly to handle an unusual situation. But because the chronic complainer and the excuse-maker in your office do basically the same things over and over, you have plenty of time to prepare some surprising statement for the next time you face them.

You can sometimes stir up useful ideas by asking yourself what you would do differently if you weren't so frustrated or angry about your situation. Or what if you suddenly had decided to quit this job—what would you then feel free to try? Imagining what you could do then might break your old mold of thinking and produce a good solution.

Two vice presidents in two entirely different businesses had exactly the same problem with their bosses. Both presidents went on tirades and threatened demotion, termination, or a transfer to some remote office if the vice presidents didn't shape up. Both vice presidents were performing well; this was just their presidents' way of keeping people working hard.

Each VP figured out how to get his boss to change his style—but they chose entirely different strategies. The first remedy isn't for the fainthearted but, outlandish though it was, it worked. It may trigger another idea that is workable (and perhaps as much fun) for you.

The first VP had gone home one evening ready to turn in his resignation the following day. As he told me: "I sat down on the couch beside my five-year-old daughter and watched cartoons with her, too tired and discouraged to do anything else. Then something on the screen caught my eye. Here was little Yosemite Sam—you know, that stubby little cartoon cowboy with the red handlebar mustache, huge hat, and the six-shooters on his hips—losing another round to the big bad man. I laughed out loud when he jumped up and down in frustration. I knew just what he felt like. Suddenly I had this idea. I knew what I could do about my boss. I was going to quit anyway, so what the hell?

"The next day I got a chance to try out my new plan. My boss called me in and began one of her tirades. I let her bellow for about a minute and then suddenly I clenched my fists and stomped my feet just like Yosemite Sam, and in Sam's voice I said, 'Ooooh, that makes me soooooo mad!' Well, she was speechless! I then calmly told her I would handle her complaint and that I'd get back to her later. She said 'Fine,' shuffled some papers on her desk, and I left. And that was that. She didn't yell at me after that—ever! I couldn't believe it. I was almost disappointed: I couldn't wait to turn Yosemite Sam loose on her again. But she never gave me the chance. Oh, she continued to chew out everyone else, but not me. I didn't need to turn in my resignation."

Sometimes a dramatic problem is worth a dramatic solution. And doing the unexpected can work wonders. The second VP also did the unexpected—he just picked a less sensational but equally successful solution. He asked for a meeting with the president. Then he simply stated that when the president threatened to fire or demote him, it made him unable to think clearly and less able to work. His threats were demotivating and not helping him get his job done. The president sat quietly for a moment. Then he said, "Well, it works for others, but I guess it doesn't work for you." And he quit threatening that vice president.

The two vice presidents had different approaches to an abrasive boss and both approaches worked. Outrageous solutions can work, as can calm and logical ones. All you have to do is:

> Think about what unexpected action you could take that would surprise the other person and throw him off his game.

There's another way to trigger new solution ideas—find out what's blocking your creativity.

7. CHALLENGE YOUR STORY

In chapter two you learned that we tell ourselves stories to explain why people behave as they do. For instance, if your gruff manager usually dispenses assignments with terse and incomplete instructions, you could explain her behavior by saying that she's trying to make you fail, or you could say that she is an unapproachable person. Either story could be correct. But what if she just has trouble getting her thoughts out clearly and hides her weakness with a gruff manner? If your story of malicious intent made you suspicious or resentful, you would have more trouble coming up with a simple solution, like asking questions that help her clarify the message.

So if you're stuck trying to figure out how to get someone to change, look at your story about that person. What type of solution does it prompt you to use? If that solution hasn't worked, then your story has probably sidetracked you. The quickest way to get back on track is to describe again the actual problem: Who does what to whom, and how that behavior is a problem. Once you're focused again, you can pick any one of the methods in this chapter to find an appropriate solution for your situation. So if you're stuck:

> Challenge your story and refocus on the problem.

And just as you have a story about others, you will also have one about yourself, one that could stop you from trying a new solution.

8. CONSIDER "OFF-LIMITS" OPTIONS

All of us live by certain specific rules of conduct that we respond to as automatically as a red traffic light. Many such rules,
usually acquired in childhood, work well to smooth human inter-
action. (Don't talk with your mouth full, never tell a lie, say what
you mean and mean what you say, always finish what you start,
be prompt/polite/tidy, anything worth doing is worth doing well,
and so on.) But at times these useful rules can interfere with getting a difficult person to change. For example, when faced with a
bully intent on some prolonged harangue, it may be appropriate
to raise your voice and interrupt. But if you were brought up
with "Keep your voice down!" and "It's not polite to interrupt,"
you may find that hard to do. Your rules kick in almost uncon-
sciously and preclude the option. If the idea does cross your
mind, you instantly discard it as improper. Thus rules that normally serve you well can inappropriately limit your options.

If you can't figure out how to get someone to change, exam-
ine the rules of conduct you're applying. There may be some
rule that you should temporarily suspend. After all, it isn't
"rude" to walk away in the midst of a conversation when you
know you'll blow up if you stay. Or maybe you should be late for
once when meeting a chronically tardy friend (or go ahead and
"impolitely" order your meal without waiting for her—creating
consequences for her for a change). Sometimes you should not
answer someone's question—like the curmudgeon from the
warehouse who uses accusatory questions to control the conversation. As you challenge your rules, you'll find times when you
may need to temporarily suspend some rule that in normal circumstances you will continue to observe.

Since your rules of conduct tend to operate automatically,

they often remain hidden from conscious thought. You can expose some of them by finishing the following sentences. The answers will sketch out your story about yourself:

- I'm the kind of person who never (or always) . . .
- I think of myself as someone who . . .
- I want people to say of me . . .
- When I think about trying to get this person to change, I could never . . .
- The only reasonable way to handle the situation I'm in is . . .

You now have a snapshot of some rules you live by, and a chance to reassess their usefulness. Rules have an important place in life, but few rules apply equally to all circumstances. Your rules of conduct may be holding you back from considering a perfectly good solution to a difficult dilemma.

> Question your rules of conduct.

The following is an exercise to help you invent workable solutions in spite of entrenched rules of conduct that may inhibit you.

TO CONSIDER "OFF-LIMITS" SOLUTIONS

1. List solutions that you could never see yourself doing to resolve this problem—whether the reluctance comes from your personal rules of conduct or from organizational rules.
2. Tag the solutions that are very different from your old ineffective one. Discard illegal or unethical ones.

3. Consider each of the tagged solutions and imagine actually doing it—what you would say or do and the response you might get. Don't pay too much attention to feelings of discomfort—uneasiness almost always accompanies the thought of breaking a long-standing rule.

4. Then challenge yourself about the rule that holds you back. Maybe you should ignore it in this instance. If so, give the solution a try—as long as this new solution is very different from your old ineffective one.

Maybe, though, there's something else in your way—someone's advice.

9. QUESTION THE ADVICE YOU'RE HEEDING

Well-meant advice can sometimes blind you to better solutions. For example, a respected colleague may save you a lot of grief by advising you, "Don't let Gus get the better of you." But if you find yourself constantly at loggerheads with Gus, then your colleague's advice may be making things worse, blinding you to a different story about Gus (the gruff old guy is really a softie once you get to know him) or obscuring other ways of dealing with him (maybe he values loyalty and once you prove yourself, he'll become your biggest supporter).

So another way to find new solutions is to review the advice you've heard from your boss, colleague, friend, sister, and spouse about the "right" way to get someone to change. First, forget all the advice that is another rendition of the solution you know won't work. Then consider any of the advice that is different from what you've already tried unsuccessfully—especially 180 degrees different. You don't have to implement that advice exactly the way your courageous sister or your burly colleague might. You can tailor it to fit you (but don't accidentally tailor it right back into your old comfortable but ineffective solution).

> Make sure someone's advice isn't holding you back.

10. SIGNAL A U-TURN

Signaling a U-turn is something to consider when you plan how to implement a strategy. Sometimes the new strategy you pick will be a subtle change in your behavior. At other times you'll make a major turnaround. The more dramatic your change of strategy, the more likely that you will need to set the stage for it by signaling a U-turn.

An abrupt shift in your behavior can create suspicion in the people you're trying to change, possibly making them wonder what you're up to. So providing an explanation helps them interpret your new actions positively.

Patricia, the park ranger who asked Roger to be more negative instead of less, had to explain her change of heart somehow. She did so by stating that the team needed to think more carefully about its prospective plans to save time and money in the long run, and that criticism would help accomplish that. Thus, she signaled her U-turn.

You also saw Jeanette flag a U-turn to Gwen, her abrasive peer. Jeanette's previous ineffective solution had been to urge Gwen to quit being so critical. To explain her change of direction, she told Gwen that she'd noticed that their boss treated her work with less scrutiny when Gwen lambasted it, and so she'd like Gwen to continue her criticism.

You don't always need to preface your new approach with an explanation. Often you can simply make the change and see what happens. But the more dramatic your shift in direction, the more likely you'll need to say something to short-circuit people's natural suspicion of a sudden change. Sometimes just announcing your U-turn can change the other person's behavior, as long as you don't go back to your former way of dealing with the problem.

In Summary

You've now got a tool kit filled with methods for devising new strategies. One or another of the methods should show you how to get your difficult person to change. The methods are all based on this simple rule: Stop doing more of the same and instead do something significantly different. While this model can be summarized simply, it takes a little time to master. Your new strategy often bumps up against your old commonsensical solution— your natural response to the problem. This can make you hesitant to try your new strategy.

The normal apprehension about doing something different reminds me of a first kayaking lesson, which consists of learning how to turn the kayak upright when you roll it over. Since you are fastened into the kayak and hang upside down underwater when you flip over, getting upright in a hurry is not a trivial skill. The Eskimo Roll requires four steps in a particular sequence. It isn't until the fourth step that you finally get to lift your head out of the water and grab a breath of air. If you go for air sooner, you only roll over again. Since every fiber of your body wants to poke your head out first, not last, this technique forces you to fight your common sense. Until you win that struggle, you keep finding yourself staring at the bottom of the lake, turning blue. But when you finally go against your logic, you pop upright in seconds. The Eskimo Roll is simple; getting yourself to go against your natural inclinations takes practice.

This three-step process for changing difficult behavior also takes practice. After all, you are teaching yourself to think in a new way about getting people to change: to think in terms of the dance—how your reactions can inadvertently reinforce rather than discourage irritating behavior. You're teaching yourself a new way to define the problem, and demanding that your active mind settle down and focus on the primary issues. So it's OK if the first new solution you try doesn't work. You will discover how to zero in better on the next effort. And each time you stop and think through what's reinforcing the unwanted behavior, you get closer to using this method effortlessly.

TWELVE

Ready, Set, Go:
Persuading Yourself
to Try Something New

Sometimes we don't want to try a new solution even though the current one clearly isn't working. We're like the old country couple heading off to visit distant kin. They drive along happily for several hours until Ma looks at the map and suddenly tells Pa that he's driving in the wrong direction. Pa says, "Uh-huh," and continues driving. Ma waits a minute, then says, "Why aren't you turning around?" Pa replies, "Because we're making such good time."

Like Pa, we can get invested in our strategy and become reluctant to cut our losses. Justifying our solution can become an art form as we craft stories to explain away its failure. As John Weakland of MRI said, "We are all capable of expending a good deal of rather creative energy trying to prove ourselves right even when the evidence clearly indicates that our efforts have failed." ("There's nothing wrong with our marketing plan. It's the best we've ever had, designed by the best team we've ever put together. Customers just never know what they really want. It's those Generation Xers who mess up the stats.")

Talking yourself into trying a new strategy can sometimes be a challenge. You may be highly motivated to get someone to change. You may be absolutely clear that what you've been doing so far hasn't worked. You may even know exactly what to do differently to get that change. But you find yourself hesitating, postponing, equivocating, and in the meantime continuing time after time to handle your troublesome situation in the same unproductive way. What's going on?

What's going on is human nature at its most cantankerous having its way with you. It takes the form of thoughts that play through your mind like an audiotape—but you don't hear these thoughts clearly. Instead, every time you get ready to try your new solution, the subliminal tape runs and tells you not to. But if you've planned your new solution carefully, you need to short-circuit the tape that stops you from acting.

While each of us has our own particular reasons for hesitating (our own special tape), there are several common variations. To figure out how to turn off your tape, read through the following examples and pick the one that most echoes the thought that makes you hesitate. After each tape you'll find some thoughts for countering the tape's paralyzing effect.

1. THE "SUNK COSTS" TAPE

As you consider your new game plan, the thought that makes you hesitate sounds something like this: "I've already invested all this time (worry, effort, money) in my old game plan. I can't just abandon what I've been doing. As the saying goes, 'If at first you don't succeed, try, try again.' After all, maybe I just haven't tried hard enough or long enough. What I've been doing should have worked, so I'd better give it a little more time."

On the Other Hand:

It can seem like admitting that you've wasted time or made a mistake to drop your old strategy. But you haven't. You've experimented with a plausible solution that didn't pan out. Learning by trial and error isn't wasting time—as long as you learn and move on. Or as W. C. Fields put it: "If at first you don't succeed, try, try again . . . then give it up. There's no use being a damn fool about it." After all, you're only giving up an ineffective solution and substituting one that is much more likely to work.

Perhaps your tape sounds a little different, and the "Things Could Be Worse" message holds you back.

2. THE "THINGS COULD BE WORSE" TAPE

When this tape plays, your nervousness about trying something new usually grows: "What if I make things worse? What if I do something that makes the other person mad or embarrassed or sad (or quit). Maybe I should just learn to live with the problem. I'd better not try anything too different."

On the Other Hand:

It's true that you can never be totally sure what will happen if you do something different. Fixing one problem can, in turn, change other conditions, so looking ahead is a useful exercise. Ask yourself: How likely is it that fixing your current problem will create a new one, and, if likely, how important or severe would the new problem be? You can then decide how you would handle this new challenge if it did occur.

You could also make things worse if you haven't thought things through and just intend to wing it. So hesitate a moment longer while you make sure you're on the right track. Think about that new solution that you're worried might make things worse. Is it actually new, or just more of the same old theme? Is it the outcome of your thoughtful planning, or just what you wish you could get away with? For example, if you are holding back from "telling Sam off," you're probably acting wisely. Let your planning point out the appropriate new solution. Then give it a try. A good experiment is worth a thousand "I wonders."

3. THE "MAKE LOVE NOT WAR" TAPE

When you're ready to finally confront someone about a problem, thoughts like these may hold you back: "I can't confront her now with her poor performance (or disruptive team behavior or lack of cooperation). After all, she's had such a rotten upbringing (or bad luck), the poor thing. She just couldn't take it. Maybe with a little more understanding she'll come around."

On the Other Hand:
Taking the time to understand others' problems often pays off. Many people come around with a little understanding. But sometimes people start counting on others' understanding instead of taking responsibility for the trouble they create.

If your understanding has reaped no change in someone's disruptive or nonproductive behavior, then perhaps you need to try something new. Some people need structure in order to succeed—timetables, deadlines, checkups, progress-report meetings. Being firm can do them a real service. Sometimes they need an ultimatum—something they can lean on securely as they rediscover their own internal strength. Then, with that help, they get some progress under their belts and can move to developing the self-confidence that comes with success.

It is hard to see that sometimes being firm and direct with someone is the kindest thing you can do. Don't be surprised if you find yourself hesitating. Not everyone is willing to do it, even when they know it would succeed.

4. THE "I GOTTA BE ME" TAPE

When you contemplate a significant change in your approach to someone—for example, creating consequences instead of continuing futilely to urge change—this voice echoes in your brain: "What I've been doing is honest—telling them what I think, letting them know what they should change. I can't change my tune. This is ME. This is the way I am. I can't be anyone else. To try something different—well, I'd come across as a phony."

On the Other Hand:
Of course you have to be you. You shouldn't give that up for a minute, as you'd come across falsely if you did. But everyone learns, grows, and discovers new facets of themselves throughout their lives. You can be true to yourself and still test new techniques and methods for dealing with difficulties. Many things come with practice, and trying something different doesn't make you a phony.

5. THE "I HAVE TO DO EVERYTHING PERFECTLY" TAPE

There's a top sergeant inside your head who drills: "You have standards to uphold. There are right ways and wrong ways to do things, and the world is a better place for it. The way you've been approaching this problem is the right way to do it, and if it doesn't work, then maybe that person can't change anyway."

On the Other Hand:

Standards are important guides for correct behavior and should be followed. But how you apply that standard calls for good judgment. It's like the judgment required in dealing effectively with children. One child may be deaf to all but the loudest rebuke, and another collapses in tears at the slightest frown. Correcting the child is the standard; how you do it is where judgment comes into play.

Use the same principle when you're trying to get someone to change. Stick to your standards, but allow yourself the flexibility to choose an effective approach for each situation. Allow yourself to adjust your methods as experience teaches you what doesn't work.

6. THE "YOU'RE NOT READY YET" TAPE

This tape unravels all your planning by playing on your feelings: "I'll know when the time is right to try something new. I'll feel confident and assured and eager. Since I'm still nervous or unsure, it would be better to wait until I feel ready."

On the Other Hand:

Occasionally it makes sense to wait, but not all that often. Confidence comes from success—from trying a new approach and seeing it work. Don't let your nervousness dictate. Change your actions first and your feelings will follow, not the other way around. As a wise person once said, *scared* is just *excited* that doesn't know what to do with itself.

Just Do It

Don't worry too much about getting your new solution wrong. You were getting it wrong before, and, though frustrated, you survived. If your new effort doesn't work initially, all you have to face is more of the same frustration as before as your manager continues to micromanage, your son continues to come home late, and you continue to procrastinate. But that's the good news because you get another shot at fixing it, and another and another—until you tweak your new strategy into one that breaks up the more-of-the-same dance. You'll get it right. Just have a laugh and keep learning. As that oft-quoted philosopher Anonymous once said, "Blessed are we who can laugh at ourselves, for we shall never cease to be amused."

THIRTEEN

Stick with a Winning Game: How to Keep a Problem Solved

As you work with this model, you may be surprised by how quickly you succeed. In fact, you may get results so quickly that you overlook them and keep on struggling to fix what you've already fixed. I have often heard people say how discouraged they were because nothing had changed. Then, as we talked further, they described example after example of unmistakable progress. I suspect that, after spending so much time frustrated by someone, they found it hard to believe that things could turn around so quickly. Fran, the MIS supervisor of a Los Angeles engineering firm, was typical. This follow-up interview about Kendra, her manager, demonstrates this all too common oversight:

> LUCY: "When we last met you were frustrated with Kendra's habit of going around you to give your employees assignments. Priorities changed without your knowing it, and work that you were counting on didn't get done. How do things stand now?"

FRAN: "My manager is so frustrating. She'll never change. Now she's asked me to join a committee. Where does she think I'll find the time?"

LUCY: "Before we move to that topic, I'm curious about what happened with your original problem. As I recall, you had planned to alert Kendra to the problems she creates by directly assigning work to your people. We had talked about your getting her to keep you in the loop, or better yet, for her to go through you. Did you take an opportunity to try that?"

FRAN: "Yes I did. It turned out that Kendra had no idea how often she dropped extra assignments on my group, which amazed me. But as soon as she saw a written list I'd prepared for her, she realized immediately how this was throwing my unit off schedule. Now that you mention it, she actually hasn't assigned anything to my team lately without letting me know first. And she's not giving us extra work nearly as often."

LUCY: "That's good news. How long has this change been going on?"

FRAN: "I guess about three weeks. This committee she wants me on—it's supposed to address the work-flow bottle-necks in the division. Now that I think about it, fixing the bottlenecks could mean fewer rush jobs to juggle. That would be nice."

Like many people in this fast-paced world, Fran had turned her attention to current concerns and hadn't realized she was no longer battling the same old problem. Her manager had already significantly changed her behavior and was even working on a long-range solution to the division workload problem.

When we jump to the next problem without noticing our progress on the last one, we don't learn how we succeeded and therefore what we should continue to do. We also lose the lift to our spirits that success can bring. Your manager may not be perfect, but if she's better, celebrate!

Great Expectations

Some of us don't notice the results of our new strategy because we expect transformation—preferably instantaneous—and so incremental improvement simply doesn't register with us. Mary, an eager young attorney in a large Toledo law firm, called me one day very disappointed that Raymond, another lawyer in the firm, was still treating her as spitefully as ever. "Your solution didn't work!" she said. I asked Mary how long she had tested it. She answered, "Two days." I suggested giving the solution at least a two-week run before declaring it a success or a failure. I warned Mary not to expect any major shift in Raymond's behavior during that time but rather to watch for subtle signs of progress—a nod in the hallway, eye contact in a meeting, a conversation without barbs. Two weeks later Mary called to say things were much better—a long way from perfect, but definitely improving. She had begun to notice Raymond's tentative movements toward peace. When she focused on small indicators of progress, she could see that her new strategy was working and that she should stick with it.

Not-So-Great-Expectations

Unlike Mary's expectations of instant success, some people anticipate a long and drawn-out struggle. Should change occur rapidly, people with this expectation discount the results and keep hammering away.

Gloria, a manager with a Texas oil company, believed that change comes about through prolonged and arduous effort. She had hired Michael for his extensive experience as a project leader, but later worried that he was undercutting vital teamwork. She called me in to help her coach Michael. Gloria invited Michael to our meeting and then recited example after example of Michael's deficiencies, emphasizing how destructive his abrupt and imperious communication style had been to teamwork and how hard Gloria herself was trying to help. She stressed that Michael was fortunate to have her support in saving his career. By the end of this barrage, Michael sat with his head hanging, and I must admit I felt like doing the same. Later, in talking with his team, I learned that Michael had taken Gloria's feedback to heart long ago and had worked diligently to improve his style. His progress was impressive and the team was functioning well.

But Gloria had expected great difficulty in getting through to Michael, and she told me that, while she'd noticed quite a change in him, she didn't trust that his new behavior would last. She treated it as a fluke and, to keep him motivated, continually rehashed his old mistakes. Michael, however, getting no credit for his considerable progress, felt discouraged. Why keep trying? In frustration, he cast about for another job. So, in not recognizing and then believing her success, Gloria lost a very talented project leader who had also become a good communicator.

Tending Your Scorecard

Einstein said, "It's the theory which decides what we can observe." Both kinds of expectations—that change takes great effort or that it will be immediate—can curtail your ability to observe progress. You may dismiss the small signs of progress as inconsequential and give up or you may keep working hard to effect a change that's already happened. You may feel discouraged and change tactics, even revert to your old solution, and never notice that your new strategy was working.

To accurately assess your new solution, you need a way to gauge whether things are improving (not necessarily fixed yet, but improving). You need an answer to the question:

> What would be a *small* initial indicator that things
> are beginning to move in the right direction—
> not completely resolved but starting to improve?

Suppose that you're trying to improve your tennis serve. You've learned a new way to grip the racket and you're concentrating on hitting the ball with a sharp snap of the wrist. How would you know that this serve was better than your old one? You would keep track of whether the ball landed where you'd aimed more often, whether the ball's bounce showed that there was some spin on it. You would notice if you won more points on your serve. (You would notice if your doubles partner refused to stay at the net when you served: you know, little indicators.) In other words, you would pay attention to incremental progress. Not assessing progress is like trying the new tennis serve blindfolded, then declaring it worthless.

Progress, Not Perfection

When trying out a new strategy, you need to focus on progress, not tap your foot impatiently awaiting perfection. It's normal to

feel discouraged when someone again repeats her annoying behavior. But it's not that your manager is again late for your meeting that's significant. What's significant is that it's the first time
she's been late in three weeks and she's only five minutes late,
not her traditional half hour. It's not that your husband lost his
temper again that's significant. It's that he choked off his explosion midstream and later awkwardly mumbled an apology. It's
important to notice whether the troublesome behavior is occur-
ring less often or in a less bothersome form and to recognize the
significance of those initial small changes.

Anna, a nurse in a bustling downtown hospital in Minneapo-
lis, fortunately knew to look for clues. While she enjoyed working with Aaron, a skillful and humorous nurse, his prima donna
tendencies were a little hard to take. He never offered to do anything extra for anyone, talked a good deal about himself, and
usually offered his good ideas in a condescending manner. One
day he made a flippant comment about Anna's work that stung
her deeply. She brooded for a couple of days, then decided to
talk with him.

Anna sat down with Aaron and told him specifically what he
had said that had bothered her, and what she wanted in the future from him so they could maintain a good working relationship. Aaron was stunned and declared that he hadn't intended to
hurt her. After their talk, he never mentioned the subject again
and for several days was reserved, almost pouting, around Anna.
Disappointed, she felt she'd stuck her neck out for nothing.

Then two weeks later she noticed that, for the first time,
Aaron cleaned up his own coffee-break mess. Not only that, he
made a fresh pot of coffee. While making coffee wasn't the same
as keeping a tight rein on his flippancy, it was in the ballpark—
paying attention to the needs of others—and certainly new behavior for Aaron.

At first it didn't seem significant. But rather than dismissing it, Anna realized that Aaron was making an effort to change. Granted, his initial step was dinky (and, yes, something he should have been doing all along). But many people start cautiously down the road to change, and if they don't get run over, they'll keep walking down that road. Look for the slightest movement in the direction of change. It counts.

Richard Terrell, my husband, has been a high school teacher for many years. He is convinced that teenagers—notorious for doling out gratitude and praise like most cats offer affection—teach you to gauge success with the smallest of indicators. When I visited his campus, a sophomore who hadn't looked at me or talked to me last month still wouldn't look at me. But that day he politely ventured, "How are you?" The sixteen-year-old who had scoffed and walked away when I spoke last year at Career Day stood nearby this year (with an aloof stance, of course), obviously listening to my speech. As my husband pointed out, that's what progress looks like. If you don't notice the little things, you will miss the clues that tell you to keep doing what you're doing.

It's Working! Now What?

When your new solution is working, stick with it. When Kevin told Carol, his co-trainer, to take as much time as she wanted with her lectures and this new solution got her back on schedule, he itched to say, "See? Isn't the training going more smoothly now that you're on schedule?" But this would have been a regression to his old dance steps. Tempting though it may have been, he needed to avoid saying anything that sounded like the old routine of urging her to stick to the schedule. Indulging in the old solution would have sent Carol an engraved invitation to revert to her irritating behavior.

Stick with a winning game. For instance, when Carol came up to Kevin one day and asked to see his copy of the schedule, he didn't have one and said, "I didn't bring one. Just go have a good time." Several days later when Carol said with pride, "Look. I'm right on schedule," Kevin responded, "Well, shoot. Now if I blow my lecture, I won't have an excuse. I can't blame it on being short of time." He stuck to his winning game and Carol laughed and stuck to the schedule.

If you succeeded in getting someone to change by directly confronting her behavior, then continue to address the problem. You could comment on progress, as in: "Kendra, I appreciate your letting me know in advance about extra assignments for my unit. It has really helped me balance the workload." Continued feedback would be part of this winning strategy and would keep you from returning to your old ineffective solution—silent avoidance.

In Summary

People can and do change, sometimes quite rapidly. That's not the hard part of change. It's not as hard for people to change as it is for us to let them change—to perceive that change is indeed taking place, to recognize the significance of the initial steps in the process, and to realize that the problem behavior is not the same as before. I suspect that after we've been stuck dealing with a difficult person for a period of time, disappointed and frustrated by our inability to get them to change, we protect ourselves from further disappointment by not allowing ourselves to hope. When trying out a new solution, some healthy skepticism is probably a smart move. But it's best to balance that with actively observing the results of your new efforts. You have to keep score to determine whether your strategy is on the right track.

That's why choosing small indicators lets you observe the first steps of change.

And don't forget to prepare for success—what you'll say and do to reinforce it—so that when your new plan works, you can stick with your winning game.

FOURTEEN

If It Didn't Work:
Troubleshooting Your Plan

Not every new solution you try will work perfectly the first time, particularly while you're still getting used to this new approach to problems. While it's discouraging when a strategy misses the mark, it can be useful. When the 169th filament didn't work in Thomas Edison's lightbulb, his assistant called it another failure. "No," said Edison, "we now know 169 ways that don't work." If you take the time to assess what went wrong, you won't need 169 trials to adjust your strategy and make it work.

To troubleshoot your strategy and determine your next step, take a look at the summary of the steps of this model on pages 195–97. See if there are any steps you skipped or gave short shrift to. Pay special attention to the following, as they are the places where people often go astray.

- HAVE YOU DEFINED YOUR PROBLEM CLEARLY
  AND SPECIFICALLY?

Rushing through the definition stage is the most common cause of trouble. Since you are defining problems in an unfamiliar way, you have to carefully spell out *who* is doing *what* to *whom,* and *how* that is a problem. Check to make sure you've described specific behaviors and have discarded useless conjectures ("If only he would stop and think first . . .") and speculations ("She must be bucking for a promotion") and labels (She's "unfair").

- DID YOU ADDRESS THE QUESTION "HOW IS
  THIS BEHAVIOR A PROBLEM?"?

This question is frequently skipped, yet it's the one that focuses you on the central problem. If you ignored the *how* of your problem, you may have found yourself working on a huge problem, like trying to transform the office ogre into Mister Rogers. Go back and describe the particular problem that someone's annoying habit creates and you'll have a good chance of getting him to stop it.

- DID YOU PICK YOUR MAIN CONCERN?

Maybe you accomplished the change you sought but your success brought little relief. If so, you probably fixed a tangential issue instead of the one that most bothered you. But that's not so bad. You can use what you learned in fixing the smaller problem to craft a solution for the one that matters. At the very least, it was good practice. Return to the definition stage and figure out what specifically is giving you the most grief. Ask your-self: If you could fix only one thing and had to live with the rest, what would you choose? Start there.

- IS YOUR NEW SOLUTION THE OPPOSITE OF,
  OR SIGNIFICANTLY DIFFERENT FROM,
  YOUR OLD ONE?

People often stay in their comfort zone by choosing a new so-lution only slightly different from the one they've tried over and over. But that new solution could simply have been a variation on the same old ineffective solution. Your ineffective solution re-ally does perpetuate the unwanted habits and so you really do have to completely change your part in the dance. Take another look at your list of ineffective solutions and make sure you know what type of solution you must avoid.

Be aware that just changing your manner is not necessarily changing your solution. "I stopped being nice about reminding him to get his report in on time and I really let him have it." It's the same solution, just a different delivery. Different solutions would be, for instance, to tell him to take all the time he wants or to set up consequences instead of continuing to urge change.

- DID YOU CHOOSE AN ACTIVE NEW SOLUTION
  OR DID YOU JUST STOP DOING THE OLD ONE?

"Well, I finally just gave up on him. Now I never say any-thing when he contradicts the directive he gave only yesterday." This is not an active solution. Merely stopping what you were in-effectively doing before won't solve your problem. But it's a great first step. Go back and figure out what you will do next.

- DID YOU DO IT "RIGHT"?

Sometimes it isn't your new strategy that is flawed, but your delivery. What tone of voice did you package your message in? People listen to your tone of voice as much as to your words. For instance, asking calmly, "What do you expect me to do?" is one message. The same words with an exasperated tone, "What DO you expect me to DO!" send a significantly different signal.

- DID YOU PAY ATTENTION TO INITIAL SIGNS OF CHANGE, HOWEVER SMALL?

Are you sure your solution failed? This may seem an odd question, but sometimes the problem that you set out to fix is indeed fixed. You've just moved on to the next problem without crediting the last success. For instance, your manager no longer threatens you, but he continues to threaten others. Did your solution fail? Not if the problem you set out to fix was how he treated you. His behavior toward others is a different problem. Or maybe you got your director to stop barging into your office screaming about deadlines and ruining your concentration, but she still frets and wrings her hands in staff meetings. Her staff-meeting demeanor is a different problem. The one you set out to remedy is fixed. I don't mean to suggest that the other problems don't matter. You may choose to tackle them next. But if the problem you wanted to resolve is fixed, your solution worked. Before you tackle the next one, pause at least a moment to relish your success.

● ● ●

These questions will help you troubleshoot your strategy. Also, as you evaluate your success, there are a couple of additional things to consider.

Letting Go

There may be times when you've gotten your colleague to completely stop some bothersome behavior but you just can't leave well enough alone. You may still harbor resentments since you'd endured her annoying habits for so long. You may want to get even, or at the very least thump on her until she admits that she has sinned. Tempting though this is, you are likely to lose what you'd gained. That's what Jamie did.

Jamie finally confronted her co-worker Francie about her incessant bragging. Francie was caught completely by surprise, but after thinking about it, her surprise turned to chagrin as she realized she did brag a good deal. She figured that it would take some doing to break such an ingrained habit and promised to work on it. A couple of days later, Francie asked Jamie to read the game plan she'd jotted down, to make sure she'd accurately understood what Jamie meant and to see if Jamie thought her plan would take care of the problem.

Jamie responded, but unfortunately not to Francie's request. Instead she lectured her, telling Francie that she acted from an inferiority complex and an overwhelming need for attention. She told Francie that she should simply realize how talented she was and stop seeking center stage. Rather than recognizing that Francie was willing to change, Jamie acted like she still needed to convince her. Francie was hurt by Jamie's comments, then she was sad, then livid. Jamie lost all the ground she had won by not noticing that she'd succeeded. It was as if she were still so geared for battle that she charged right through Francie's white flag.

It's not always easy to acknowledge that your difficult person has actually changed and to let go of old resentments. You can't stop yourself from wanting to get even, as that desire seems to be a default setting on the standard human being. But you can recognize the desire and stop yourself from acting on it. Freedom of choice, thank heavens, is also a default setting.

In the long run, the best way to get even is to privately bask in the knowledge that you got someone to stop driving you crazy. So sit back and enjoy the lingering satisfaction of success.

Awareness Doesn't Cause Change

There is one more pothole to avoid on the road to success: the notion that awareness alone will bring about change. People with such beliefs work hard to make sure their spouse or children or employees are fully aware of their flaws and how they cause others distress. Then, since they feel they've done their part, they sit back and expect the distressing behavior to disappear. Sometimes this works; some people are quite willing to change once bad habits are brought to their attention. But if that doesn't work, the chances of awareness alone leading to change are slim indeed. For instance, we all know someone who complains about being overweight and declares that he intends to lose weight. We know that he is fully aware that the doughnut in his hand is filled with calories. We've heard him say repeatedly that once he breaks his diet, he gets discouraged and goes on a binge. Then we watch him devour the doughnut and lick his fingers. So much for awareness.

Awareness is a shiny new Mercedes with no motor parked in

your driveway. You can admire it, polish it, sit in it, and brag about it, but it won't take you anywhere. To get somewhere with changing troublesome behavior, you must change what you do about the problem and stop counting on awareness to do the trick.

This can work in even seemingly hopeless cases. A woman in her thirties, diagnosed as schizophrenic, had spent years in a mental institution. From time to time, with little or no provocation, she would assault a staff member. The staff would, at most, put her in seclusion for a day. One day she hit a nurse who was new to the institution. The nurse, feeling this was no way to be treated, filed assault and battery charges. The judge who heard the case pronounced the woman guilty and imposed a penalty, a small fine. Within three months, the woman had pulled herself together and was out of the hospital. When asked what created such a dramatic turnaround, she cited the lawsuit: "No one had ever taken me seriously before. Until then, nothing I did had ever mattered." Years of psychiatric "awareness" hadn't helped her. But when the nurse and the judge treated her as a person responsible for her actions, this change in their behavior gave her back her life.

Some Things Can't Be Changed

You can't change everything about everyone. But you don't need to. Often all you really need is to get someone to modify an irritating habit. Your perfectionist boss will never give up poring over details, but you might be able to get him to do it less often, or alter how he tells you of his concerns, or fix whatever other specific problem his detail mania creates. Barbara, a quality-assurance specialist in a Los Angeles medical devices manufacturing plant, was so disheartened that she was ready to quit. No matter how hard she worked, her new manager always found flaws in her work. And when she fixed those, he found more. She had loved her job but now dreaded going to work. She willingly acknowledged that her manager was very good at details and that she often found his comments and insights useful. But when everything was ready to go—the speech written and practiced, all the slides prepared—and then he pointed out some detail, it infuriated her. Worse yet, she lost confidence in her presentation and her performance suffered.

Barbara and her manager both knew he wouldn't quit working the details, so they figured out how to make the best use of his talent while diminishing its drawbacks. They agreed that she would show him only the first two drafts of her work and she would gratefully accept his comments and suggestions. But after that, she was on her own. If he slipped up and pointed out details late in the game, she had the right to tell him the Suggestions Window was closed, and to disregard his comments. Did he change? He is still a details guy, but now they use his habit at appropriate times and it has become an asset. Barbara considered that a substantial change.

FIFTEEN

Speeding Along the
Learning Curve:
And Let the Changes Begin

You now have all the information you need to get that cranky boss to quit yelling, that whiny employee to come to work on time, and even that wonderful spouse to balance the checkbook. With a little practice you will zip through this three-step change process and know exactly how to get them to change. It will take practice because, as Sherlock Holmes said to Watson, "You look but you do not see." Until you get the hang of this, you will see motives and reasons for people's behavior instead of actual behaviors—*who* does *what* that creates *what* problem and *what* you have done to try and change the situation. However, there are some shortcuts to speed you along the learning curve.

If initially you work carefully, step by step, through this process, you will master it quickly. It can help to write down your problem so you can see what information you may be missing or what step you skipped. For instance, you may be clear that you always feel like a fool after a meeting with your manager, but you can't pinpoint what it is precisely she does that triggers the feeling. Write down all the steps that you know (she says X, then you say Y, then she . . . , then you . . .) up to the point that your memory becomes cloudy. You can now make use of the one advantage of recurring troublesome behavior: It recurs. You'll have another chance to see what your manager does that trips you up. The next time you meet with her, you will know at what stage to pay particular attention.

Don't try to get her to change at this point—you're not ready. Just try to see and hear what actually occurs. If your problem with her happens in staff meetings, you might ask a colleague to notice when you begin acting sheepish or suddenly go silent (or whatever you do when you feel like a fool) and ask him to note what your manager did or said. These observations should flesh out the definition of the problem and give you the information you need to figure out a solution.

Use the Buddy System

If you want to catch on to this model even more quickly, work with a friend or colleague who listens reasonably well. You can take turns working on each other's problems. Someone else's problem is usually easier to define than your own since you aren't emotionally involved.

Since this method focuses on changing your solutions and can seem counterintuitive, you'll need to cue your friend on how to help if he doesn't know the model. If you can get him to read this book, more the better. But if not, tell him clearly what information you need him to listen for as you talk about the problem: 1) who, what, to whom, and how; and 2) the basic repetitive theme in your ineffective solutions—the basic message you've been ineffectively trying to convey about what your troublesome person should or should not do, should or should not feel. If you are trying to break a personal habit, your friend would listen for what you've been repeatedly telling yourself about what you should or should not do or feel.

When you have that theme identified, figure out its opposite or something very different that will break up the more-of-the-same dance. Then together brainstorm ways to implement that new solution.

The following will help make your work together productive. Whoever's taking the role of consultant should review these tips.

SOME TIPS FOR HELPING SOMEONE WITH A PROBLEM

- DO go through the three-step process step by step.
- DO listen and probe for the facts: descriptions of behavior—who does and says what.
- DO focus on the problem that most bothers your colleague, even if a different aspect of the problem would bother you more.
- DO make sure the new solution is the opposite of the old one, or very different.
- DO help invent ways to implement the new solution. Brainstorming helps here.
- DO note that problems can seem simplistic from an observer's viewpoint so:
  - DON'T jump to giving advice without knowing what solutions have already been tried and should be avoided.
  - DON'T empathize so much with your friend

("You poor thing. How do you stand it!") that
you inadvertently inflame emotions and make
the problem seem even bigger.

- DON'T summarize in ways that bleed hope
  from the process ("This sounds impossible;
  your manager is a jerk.") Stick to the facts.

- DO carefully follow the process, step by step.

Grading Yourself on the Curve

You won't win them all. Sometimes you won't get someone to
change because you're simply out of your league. If you're playing chess against the world champion, Anatoly Karpov, you
know you're going to lose. You may as well relax, enjoy the
game, and learn some new moves to use later with someone
closer to your level. If your CEO is renowned for terrifying even
the skilled politicians in the company, then don't expect to handle him with grace and style the first time he tests your mettle.
(Give it a good try, but don't expect to come away unscathed.)

Even when you don't get someone to change exactly as you'd
wished, you can still chalk up a win by studying what didn't
work. Then you can prepare a better strategy should you run into
a similar problem again.

And sometimes just the review itself will bring you relief. A
friend of mine told me that she went from rage to relaxation in
five minutes—just by reviewing how her colleague had duped
her again. She thought she had figured this man out the first time
he'd run his number on her and believed she knew how to respond the next time, but clearly and painfully she was wrong.
She harrumphed around her office for a while, then settled down
to review step by step what had occurred between her colleague

and herself. Suddenly she could see what each had done. She could hear again what he had said that had triggered her old useless reaction.

My colleague then figured out what she could do differently the next time. To her surprise her anger immediately disappeared. She then realized that her anger came from feeling helpless to protect herself. Once she knew which maneuver invited her into their more-of-the-same dance and how to avoid getting hooked, she wasn't helpless anymore. She relaxed and actually found herself almost looking forward to the next round with him.

A failure is a failure only if you don't figure out what went wrong. Everything else is learning. So debrief each situation and grade yourself on the curve—the learning curve.

A Final Thought

Throughout this book I've given examples of how this change-your-solution approach to difficult problems can work, mainly to make the method clear. I don't intend this to be an inspirational book; inspiration only goes so far and dissipates quickly. Rather, this is meant as a practical guidebook, and probably not the final word on the challenge of addressing difficult problems. For that matter, it is less a guidebook for solving problems than it is for solving solutions. I would hope that you would use it as a reference book when you run into a problem that "won't go away." And finally, I would hope you have a little fun exploring and trying out new ideas.

Postscript

I'd like to hear about your experiences with this method—what you tried, what worked, what you learned. Please send your letters to:

Lucy Gill
P.O. Box 394
Coulterville, CA 95311

A Summary of the Steps

1. WHAT IS THE PRIMARY PROBLEM?

Who is doing
   what that presents a problem,
      to whom, and
         how is this behavior a problem?

What is your main complaint, the issue that bothers you the most or will get you the most mileage if you fix it first? If you could solve only one of your current problems and had to live with the rest, which one would you pick?

Troubleshoot your definition. Have you described behaviors that can be seen or heard? Make sure you have:

- Specific descriptions of what people actually say and do in the course of the problem—not reasons or explanations for why the problem exists or speculations about people's motives.

- Actual descriptions of behavior, not labels for behavior.
  Translate labels like "He is rude" into behavior descriptions such as "He interrupts when I am speaking."
- Descriptions of the problem, not statements about what
  you think should be done about the problem. Translate solution ideas into a description of the problem by
  asking yourself what problem your solution is intended to
  solve.
- A statement of how the troublesome behavior is a problem. What specific problem does the described behavior
  cause?

2. WHAT ARE YOU DOING ABOUT THE PROBLEM NOW?

What unsuccessful solutions have you tried?

What is the theme of those unsuccessful attempts to resolve the problem—the basic statement you are making to yourself or to others about what you (or they) should or should not do, should or should not feel?

Were there any temporary successes in your efforts to solve the problem?

3. WHAT DO YOU NEED TO DO INSTEAD?

What would be the opposite of what you are doing unsuccessfully now, or something that would be a substantial shift in direction from your previous efforts? What, if you did it, would stop you from repeating your current ineffective solution?

What will you say and do differently to implement your new solution? Do you need to introduce or explain your change of behavior in any way?

What indicators of progress will you watch for—small initial changes that will tell you things are beginning to move in the right direction, that the problem is beginning to improve?

Bibliography

Bramson, Robert. *Coping with Difficult Bosses.* New York: Carol Publishing Group, 1992.

Bramson, Robert. *Coping with Difficult People.* New York: Dell Publishing, 1981.

Covey, Stephen. *The Seven Habits of Highly Effective People: Powerful Lessons in Personal Change.* New York: Fireside Books, 1989.

de Shazer, Steve. *Keys to Solutions in Brief Therapy.* New York: Norton, 1985.

Fisch, Richard, John H. Weakland, and Lynn Segal. *The Tactics of Change: Doing Therapy Briefly.* San Francisco: Jossey-Bass, 1982.

Huber, Charles H., and Barbara Backlund. *The Twenty-Minute Counselor.* New York: The Continuum Publishing Company, 1992.

Quick, Thomas L. *Unconventional Wisdom: Irreverent Solutions for Tough Problems at Work.* San Francisco: Jossey-Bass, 1989.

Tavris, Carol. *Anger: The Misunderstood Emotion.* New York: Simon & Schuster, 1984.

Watzlawick, Paul, John H. Weakland, and Richard Fisch. *Change: Principles of Problem Formation and Problem Resolution.* New York: Norton, 1974.

Watzlawick, Paul, Janet H. Beavin, Don D. Jackson. *Pragmatics of Human Communication: A Study of Interactional Patterns, Pathologies, and Paradoxes.* New York: Norton, 1967.

Weeks, Dudley. *The Eight Essential Steps to Conflict Resolution: Preserving Relationships at Work, at Home, and in the Community.* Los Angeles: Jeremy P. Tarcher, Inc., 1992.

Weiner-Davis, Michele. *Change Your Life and Everyone In It.* New York: Fireside Books, 1995.

Index